Prepared

For Him

Become Secure in Your Relationship with Jesus as You Prepare for Your Future Husband

Vee Summer

ISBNs: 979-8-9892014-0-2 (Paperback)
      979-8-9892014-1-9 (Digital)

Printed in the United States of America
10 9 8 7 6 5 4 3 2 1

DEDICATION

To the girl who is in the midst of waiting

Acknowledgments

Dad and Mom, thank you for being a demonstration of love to one another and teammates through some of the hardest challenges. May God bless your marriage forevermore. Thank you for praying over my future husband in faith that we will meet him someday. Thank you for supporting me as I pursue the things God has called me to do.

And to all those I have looked up to for advice, correction, and prayer. Thank you for always pointing me back to Jesus. I cherish every phone call and coffee date, and I look forward to many more!

Table of Contents

Day 1	**Day 2**	**Day 3**
Pray for Unity in Your Future Marriage	Pray for Your Future Husband to Be a Man of Encouragement	Pray for Strong Core Friendships
Pg. 13	Pg. 18	Pg. 22
Day 7	**Day 8**	**Day 9**
Pray He Will Be a Father With Godly Character	Pray for His Physical Health	Pray for Clear and Consistent Communication
Pg. 39	Pg. 43	Pg. 47
Day 13	**Day 14**	**Day 15**
Pray for His Mental Health	Pray for His Family and Extended Family	Pray He Finds Hope in His Heavenly Father
Pg. 65	Pg. 69	Pg. 73
Day 19	**Day 20**	**Day 21**
Pray He Is a Man of Prayer	Pray For Healing From Past Relationships	Pray He Is Zealous to Share the Truth of the Gospel
Pg. 90	Pg. 94	Pg. 98
Day 25	**Day 26**	**Day 27**
Pray He Will Resist Temptation	Pray That His Dependence and Trust Is in Jesus Alone	Pray for His Career and the Role He Plays Among His Coworkers
Pg. 116	Pg. 121	Pg. 125

Table of Contents

How to Use This Book

This thirty-day devotional is designed to bring us closer to Jesus as we prepare our heart for marriage. Both the Challenge and Reflection sections can be journaled to help you internalize new concepts, and in turn, will help you dig deeper. Journaling tracks your growth and ideas. May the Holy Spirit guide you.

Each day contains:

➤ A **Devotional**: firmly based on the Word of God and personal experience to encourage and teach.

➤ A **Challenge**: This would be too easy without a challenge! Let's put what we learn into practice. This is our chance to do the work and become the women our future husbands are seeking. I encourage you to go above and beyond these challenges, implementing these actions to develop new habits that can launch the course of your future in a strong and positive way.

➤ A time of **Reflection**: We will take a moment and look at our life. Where are we now? Where are we going? Where do we want to be? As you search yourself, you will step into areas that have never been examined before.

➤ **Pray About It**: We will pray specifically over each day's topic and lay our requests at Jesus's feet. Once you speak the included prayers aloud, you may also be creative with your own. Prayer changes hearts and minds!

> **Today's Scripture(s)**: Without the Word of God as our corner-stone, we would aimlessly be trying to build relationships our own way. Scripture defines our relationships. This devotional includes Bible readings to supplement your personal Bible study. Explore the verses, and memorize them to get a better understanding of what God says about relationships.

Introduction

A wife of noble character who can find? She is worth
far more than rubies. (Proverbs 31:10)

Your future husband is going to find you! You are in training to be a wife of noble character, and girl, let me tell you, you are worth far more than rubies!

It is my desire that as you read these pages, you feel secure in who you are because of who Jesus made you to be. May you be prepared for your future husband and equipped for what God has for you both. I hope you recognize that the season you are in right now is *good.* With or without a husband, you have worth. A man will never be able to define your worth—not in the way Jesus does. Be content where you are, but anticipate where you are going. It will be good because God is good!

Let's journey through this together with eternity in mind. We only have two options when it comes to eternity: heaven or hell. Choosing to become a Christian is our own personal decision. Salvation is our choice and a gift from God. A change must occur in us in order to enter into a relationship with the Lord. We must simply submit to Jesus as our Lord and Savior. Jesus told one of His disciples, "I am the way and the truth and the life. No one comes to the Father except through me." (John 14:6)

This is our opportunity to say "Yes!" to God and live our lives anticipating being with Him in heaven. Only through Jesus Christ is a firm relationship built. Knowing Jesus and abiding in Him daily will allow you to live a more abundant life that brings freedom, peace, and hope: none of which can be found in anything else. Be proud of your decision to live according to God's Word. We commit our lives to Jesus through prayer, saying, "I have decided to follow You." This decision brings us into a relationship with the Father and secures our place in heaven.

Careful consideration in choosing your husband will be the second biggest decision you ever make. Our choices matter because they lead us to a destination. Who we date is a choice. Saying yes to a proposal is a choice. *That choice is a lifelong decision.* Marriage is for a lifetime, so use wisdom in making this decision. As you wait on God, He will give you a sense of security and peace when you choose the right man.

Relationships take time, effort, and prayer. This is true for a relationship with God or a man. Our priorities need to be God first, then our spouse, then family, and then everything else. It's only when we keep God first that our relationships thrive and function in the way He intended.

> Relationships take time, effort,
> and prayer.

Let's spend this time evaluating our walk and challenge ourselves to grow in our relationship with the Lord. We'll learn how to pray for our future husband as we lean closer to the Lord. My hope is that by the end of this book, you'll be encouraged to continue seeking God and His will as He unfolds the plan He has for your life. Our goal is to have lifelong healthy and fulfilling relationships! As we place our heart in His faithful hands, He will meet with us and guide us through the process.

Day 1: Pray for Unity in Your Future Marriage

In a relationship, unity resembles a team working together to complete a common goal. It reminds me of the three-legged race I competed in when I was in the sixth grade. Your left leg is tied to the right leg of your partner or vice versa. The goal is to get to the finish line without falling. The team works together to navigate this movement individually while being tied to each other. The rope holds you together, and you must work together to determine the pace. If one tries to pull ahead, the other falls. If one slows, you both fall. If one stops, you're both halted. Marriage is like that too.

> "Haven't you read," he replied, "that at the beginning the Creator 'made them male and female,' and said, 'For this reason a man will leave his father and mother and be united to his wife, and the two will become one flesh'? So they are no longer two, but one flesh. Therefore, what God has joined together, let no one separate." (Matthew 19:4-6)
>
> Though one may be overpowered, two can defend themselves. A cord of three strands is not quickly broken. (Ecclesiastes 4:12)

The same is true for our relationships from a spiritual perspective. You are tying yourself to another person, and to get anywhere, you need to be consistently running toward the same goal at the same pace. Jesus is the cord that binds you together. The three strands in the verse above represent a man, a woman, and God.

Note in the diagram below that the One who has the power is God. He is at the top. All the sides are the same length; to move closer to your husband, you need to move closer to God. If you are both moving equally toward God, who is always at the top, you are getting closer to the finish line.

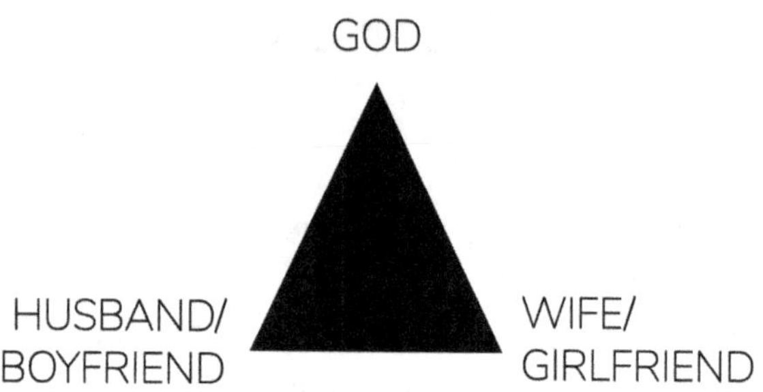

We should desire to be equally yoked with our partner, chasing God in the same way, at the same pace, at the same time. If we are equally yoked, we are seeking the Lord at the same measure. How do you know? First of all, you need to know if your partner (or the guy who asked you out) is a believer in Jesus Christ. If he is not, and you are, you are unequally yoked. Red flag.

> If we are equally yoked, we are seeking the Lord at the same measure.

It goes beyond that question though. It's also about the way you seek God. If you are spending your time in the Word, attending church, and in fellowship with other believers, and he doesn't desire to do those things or put forth the effort to experience them with you, that's another red flag. This doesn't mean he couldn't be encouraged to do those things or that he won't radically fall in love with Jesus at some point, but it is an indicator that you are not on the same page as believers right now. Spiritually, you both need to be in sync with how deeply you desire to know Christ. You want a man who truly desires to know Him and follow Him—not someone who is just checking off a religious to-do list. The

Christian walk is relational—between you and God. The way someone does life reveals that relationship.

God works in our lives in His timing and in different ways. The way God speaks to you might not be the way He speaks to your future husband. You don't know what his relationship with God is like, but you can be sure that your significant other should not be dependent on your spiritual walk to carry him to God. Additionally, you can't jump into his life with the intention of helping him grow closer to the Lord. This is not a rescue mission. That is a path he will need to take on his own. Just as you had a choice and chose to follow Jesus, the man you are interested in has the same choice before him. Be sure that he has truly made that choice.

You cannot change another person—and you will not change them—no matter how hard you try or how badly you want to do that. Only God can do that. We can't pressure God to change someone to be the way we want them to be either. That is an authority we do not hold. Just because we want someone to change (and we know Jesus is a God of change) doesn't mean it will happen, so it's important to discern whether a man is on the same spiritual page as you.

Challenge

Be intentional about the time you spend with Jesus. Determine whether you are truly pursuing Christ. Set an uninterrupted date with Jesus today for thirty minutes to read, worship, and pray. Just spend time with Him. Invite the Holy Spirit into the moment, and rest in His presence. Be aware of how you are spending your time and with whom you are spending it.

Pray About It

Lord, I pray my heart will be positioned in a way that is honoring to You. I desire to spend time with You and know more about You. I pray that my future spouse is eager to chase after You in the same way I am. Help us both to run hard toward Your promises and Your truth. Thank You for unity in marriage. I pray that You are at the center of our relationship from the beginning to the end. I pray for depth in our relationship that draws us closer to You and one another. In Jesus's name. Amen.

Today's Scriptures:

"Haven't you read," he replied, "that at the beginning the Creator 'made them male and female,' and said, 'For this reason a man will leave his father and mother and be united to his wife, and the two will become one flesh'? So they are no longer two, but one flesh. Therefore, what God has joined together, let no one separate." (Matthew 19:4-6)

Though one may be overpowered, two can defend themselves. A cord of three strands is not quickly broken. (Ecclesiastes 4:12)

Day 1 Reflection Questions

1. Do you regularly take time out of your day to be with God?

____

2. How do you include Jesus in your everyday life? How much do you crave to spend time with Him?

____

____

3. Do your actions reflect that you are drawing nearer to Christ?

____

4. Does the man you are interested in push you closer to the Lord? Do your friends?

____

5. Are you setting an example of what it looks like to be a follower of Jesus Christ? If not, how can you do so?

____

____

____

6. Have you ever tried to justify someone else's faith? Why? What are you trying to prove?

____

____

____

Day 2: Pray for Your Future Husband to Be a Man of Encouragement

Therefore encourage one another and build each other up, just as in fact you are doing. (1 Thessalonians 5:11)

As God's people, we need to be encouraged—and encourage others. Whether in our work, finances, diet, or even our gym routine, we all need an extra boost to push us through those mundane moments, off days, and temptations. We need to encourage one another and build each other up, fighting off discouragement.

> We need to encourage one another
> and build each other up.

It's easy to become discouraged. I can readily find lots of discouraging things within five minutes of waking each day. Maybe you woke up with a lingering stomachache from the night before, or you are irritable from a restless night's sleep, or your period came, and you realize it's going to be one of those days—all before crawling out of bed! Then you can't figure out what to wear, you find a new pimple erupting on your chin, and finally, you spill your coffee on your way out the door. That sounds pretty bad, but it is reality. So many aspects of our lives can be discouraging.

When our day consists of a discouraging series of events (or discouragements from the previous day are on our mind), God does not want it to stay like that. We are called to continually build each other up with encouragement, even in our own discouraging moments. We need to hear positive words of encouragement and speak them to others. Our actions can show encouragement. As women of God, we need to be contributors, not consumers. I admit it. It is easy to accept the praise and the compliments, and be exhorted myself, without doing the same for others. Guilty! We will only be consumers of encouragement if we do not pass it on to someone else. Intentionally encourage someone else today through words or actions as you pray for your future husband to be encouraged.

Encouragement is a gift. The Holy Spirit gives us the ability to encourage others—even when we don't feel like it.

> Do not let any unwholesome talk come out of your mouths, but only what is helpful for building others up according to their needs, that it may benefit those who listen. (Ephesians 4:29)

Challenge

Encourage someone today. Ask God to lay someone on your heart or show you someone in need of encouragement. Call a friend to see how they are or send a thank you note to someone who blessed you. If you see someone doing a good job today at work, school, or church, write them a note to let them know that someone noticed. If you observe someone doing something well, make it known. Encourage them to keep doing it. This may be the extra push they need to help them conquer the day.

Pray About It

Heavenly Father, give me a heart full of encouragement. Help me build others up and exhort them as I go throughout my day. Give me new ideas on how I can make someone else's day better, whether it is through words or actions. May encouragement overflow from me. Lord, I pray my future husband feels encouraged and enlightened by You and those around him today. Let him be empowered and eager to encourage people within his sphere of influence. Allow us to recognize the moments when we can contribute to praising the greatness in someone else rather than dismissing it. In Jesus's name we pray. Amen.

Today's Scriptures:

Therefore encourage one another and build each other up, just as in fact you are doing. (1 Thessalonians 5:11)

Do not let any unwholesome talk come out of your mouths, but only what is helpful for building others up according to their needs, that it may benefit those who listen. (Ephesians 4:29)

Day 2 Reflection Questions

1. Who can you encourage today?

____

____

2. How often do you take the time to encourage someone?

____

____

3. When you see something you like, do you recognize it by commenting on it? It could be as simple as an admirable personality trait, a skill that amazes you, or even an article of clothing.

____

____

4. Do you speak words of encouragement? Or do you take the easy route and move on with what you are doing without commenting?

____

____

5. How can you be a better contributor to those around you by using encouraging words?

____

____

Day 3: Pray for Strong Core Friendships

One key to a successful marriage is being part of a community of Christ-followers. Friendships with other believers are important because they will offer biblical advice and hold you accountable.

> Walk with the wise and become wise, for a companion of fools suffers harm. (Proverbs 13:20)

As Christians, we need to be very cautious when it comes to our friendships. Maybe you are still closely connected to people from high school, college, or your workplace. We need to be able to discern the influence the people around us have on our life. If we don't, it's likely we could be allowing sin into our life, become a slave to loneliness, or be hurt by the words and actions of others. Sometimes we feel the need to act a certain way with a certain group of people because they know our past. People will remember how we once were, but when Jesus stepped in, our life changed. Life should not be the same as it was. I am not the same as I was before Christ. It is okay to make it known that you are different now. It testifies of the redemptive story of Jesus when you change. This is your testimony. He is a God of change. Christ changes things for the good.

We need authentic friendships that have depth, transparency, and vulnerability.

We need authentic friendships that have depth, transparency, and vulnerability. We tend to go days without asking someone how they are navigating a troubling season or without being honest about how we are dealing with the roadblocks in our own life. Many of us stay guarded when sharing our struggles and the uncomfortable places in our heart. We quickly say we are *fine* when we are not. We need core people in whom we can confide that will provide honest and biblically supported advice.

> As iron sharpens iron, so one person sharpens another.
> (Proverbs 27:17)

If you don't have those friends, pray for them. If you already have them, hold them close and value their friendship. Friendship is a treasure to be protected. Do not shy away from letting your friends know how much you value them. As years pass, friendships weave in and out of your life. It's likely that you don't yet know the people that will be in your circle when you raise your kids, go on vacations, and with whom you will spend quality time over the next few decades. Begin to pray that these people will seek God the way you and your future spouse do, and that He will provide trustworthy people for you to grow alongside. You become what your closest five friends are. Be mindful of the voices you are allowing to speak into your life.

Challenge

As you develop relationships with people in your sphere of influence, spend quality time with them so you can really get to know each other. Invite them! Invite them to church. Invite them to coffee. Invite them to go on a walk. Invite them to do something you both have shown interest in. Step out of your comfort zone and converse with someone that shares a common interest with you. One small initial conversation could lead to a lifetime of friendship. Be prayerful about the people with whom you connect. Discern what your current friendships look like. Join a small group or Bible study, and attend church events to increase the chance of interacting with people you have never met before.

Pray About It

Heavenly Father, I pray to be surrounded by a community of people able to speak truth into my life and that of my future husband. I ask that You bring new friends into our lives, ones that will help us grow closer to You. Please provide a covering of leaders and mentors who will give us hard truths when we need them. I pray for relationships with depth. Give me patience as I wait for the people You will bring into my life. I desire authentic relationships with people I have met in the past and will meet in the future. Please bring the right people into my life. I crave healthy friendships, mentors, and leaders in my life, so prepare my heart to receive from them. Lead me to them, Lord, so we may come together and honor You. In Jesus's name. Amen.

Today's Scriptures:

Walk with the wise and become wise, for a companion of fools suffers harm. (Proverbs 13:20)

As iron sharpens iron, so one person sharpens another. (Proverbs 27:17)

Day 3 Reflection Questions

1. Other than family members, identify five people you think know the real you. Do they truly know you? Do they support you and encourage you in a credible way?

____

____

____

2. What do your friends' lives look like? Are they walking with the Lord?

____

____

3. Are your present friendships pointing you closer to God?

____

____

4. Who is present to drop everything and pray with you on your hard days?

____

____

5. Who is sharpening you? Who are you sharpening?

____

____

____

Day 4: Pray for a Man Who Is Fully Surrendered to Christ

We should be seeking a man who passionately desires a strong walk with the Lord. If he doesn't know God's love, he won't be able to love how God loves. He should be able to share his testimony too, relating how he was saved or how God is working in his life currently. Don't be afraid to ask him about his testimony. To know his heart, we should want to know what the God who created his heart has done in his life. We need to know he has been saved. This can easily be hidden in relationships. Use caution and don't assume he is a believer or was raised in the church, or even wants to have a deeper relationship with the Lord. Being able to tell where he is spiritually will help you discern if you should invest in the relationship. Be mindful of the men that you allow to have your time. We often find ourselves with someone based on butterflies, charm, or the desire to be in a relationship out of loneliness. These are feelings built on sand. Our relationships need to be built on the Rock that is solid and sturdy. Jesus is the foundation we seek.

> Therefore everyone who hears these words of mine and puts them into practice is like a wise man who built his house on the rock. The rain came down, the streams rose, and the winds blew and beat against the house; yet it did not fall, because it had its foundation on the rock. But everyone who hears these words of mine and does not put them into practice is like a foolish man who built his house on sand. (Matthew 7:24-26)

A relationship deeply rooted in faith takes time and faithful submission to God—daily submission. Through this process, we become sanctified, which means we become more like Christ. The way we live our lives should become more holy and pure. Grasp the importance of what it means to have a relationship with God. We have to deeply desire an authentic relationship with our Creator. We have to want to know about the One who knows us best. The first step toward sanctification is surrender—not just a portion of your life, but all of it—every area. Jesus needs to be allowed in every part of our heart. Ultimate surrender will lead us closer to Christ.

> May God himself, the God of peace, sanctify you through and through. May your whole spirit, soul and body be kept blameless at the coming of our Lord Jesus Christ. The one who calls you is faithful and he will do it. (1 Thessalonians 5:23-24)

A relationship deeply rooted in faith takes time and faithful submission to God—daily submission.

Challenge

Analyze the amount of surrender, submission, and effort you put into knowing Jesus. Have you surrendered all areas of your life to Him? What effort are you putting into your relationship with Him?

Get baptized! If you haven't been baptized, and you have committed your life to the Lord, there is no better time than now to do it. Baptism is a public declaration of an inward work. It is an outward representation and commitment to living your life for Christ. If you are unsure about what it is, discuss it with your pastor or another leader in your church, and pray about it. When you are ready, commit yourself to God, and the commitment to man will follow.

Marry a man who has been baptized or wants to be baptized, showing that he is actively pursuing a relationship with God. This is a decision he must make on his own—not for you and not for others.

Pray About It

Dear heavenly Father, I ask for wisdom and guidance over my future husband. Give him knowledge, understanding, and discernment for the future. Show him the importance of having a deeply rooted relationship with You. My desire is that he desires You. Allow his relationship with You to be real and divine. Motivate him and strengthen him in his relationship with You daily. I pray that he chases after opportunities to learn more about who You are. In Jesus's name. Amen.

Today's Scriptures:

Therefore everyone who hears these words of mine and puts them into practice is like a wise man who built his house on the rock. The rain came down, the streams rose, and the winds blew and beat against the house; yet it did not fall, because it had its foundation on the rock. But everyone who hears these words of mine and does not put them into practice is like a foolish man who built his house on sand. (Matthew 7:24-26)

May God himself, the God of peace, sanctify you through and through. May your whole spirit, soul and body be kept blameless at the coming of our Lord Jesus Christ. The one who calls you is faithful and he will do it. (1 Thessalonians 5:23-24)

Day 4 Reflection Questions

1. Has the man you're considering accepted Jesus Christ as his Savior? Have you?

____

____

2. Are you pursuing Christ daily?

____

3. Have you seen the faithfulness of God in your life? If so, describe a time.

____

____

____

4. Have you been baptized or thought about publicly committing your life to Christ through baptism? If not, what is holding you back?

____

____

____

____

Day 5: Pray He Is Humble

Jesus is the perfect example of a Man of humility. He was born in a stable among barn animals and placed in an uncomfortable manger in unsanitary conditions! This is the lowest circumstance of birth. How could the King of the world be welcomed so? But Jesus was born into this situation. Later, He washed the feet of His disciples to teach them humility. After that, He was beaten, cursed, and nailed to a cross by people who didn't see Him as the Messiah—without resistance. That is the God we serve.

Pride is all about itself. Self-seeking. Self-centered. Self-focused. Self-absorbed. At its root, pride seeks continual attention and demands to be at the center of everything. Pride is selfish. Pride is sin.

> God opposes the proud but shows favor to the humble.
> (James 4:6b)

In conversation, we can play the "Who Did It Better" game by exchanging our victories, each trying to one-up the other instead of listening and honestly celebrating the other person's accomplishments. What is our intention? It speaks more about our character when we celebrate others without putting our victories on display. It's better to acknowledge their accomplishments rather than try to trump them with our own. What are you working toward? Inclusion? Influence? Praise? Those things never satisfy. Our pride gets in the way of our true identity. We cannot walk in the fullness of who God created us to be if there is pride in us. Let's learn to recognize pride. If we look for it, we will find it. Once found, we can discard it and put on humility instead.

Becoming humble is a beautiful process, especially when we can admit our wrongdoings. Respect grows when we genuinely admit our failures. Humility proves we don't have it all figured out. Our imperfections are evidence that we are still in process. We are not alone. It is okay to admit we do not have it all together and show our vulnerability. Humility is recognized by God and by people. God blesses the humble. When we share the truth about ourselves, it brings about true fellowship and growth in the body of Christ.

> If I must boast, I will boast of the things that show my weakness. (2 Corinthians 11:30)

Humility can be shown in many ways: going to the Lord in prayer, worship, and praise are examples of being humble before the Lord. These allow room for the Holy Spirit to move in our life.

Selflessness is simply thinking of ourselves less often and putting others first.

Selfishness wounds relationships, while self*less*ness strengthens relationships. Selflessness is simply thinking of ourselves *less* often and putting others first. In selfishness, we think about ourselves all the time. Pride will divide. It will divide romantic relationships, friendships, and families. Yielding to others shows we support them. Humility doesn't seek recognition for the good you have done. In relationships, we need to be selfless with time, money, and even our food. Giving up things we love for someone else is a true act of humility. Seek to serve your spouse in this way. Give up your desires just as Jesus modeled for us on the cross. As we work on humility in our own life, let's pray our future husband is doing the same.

Challenge

Ask a mentor or a trusted friend if they see pride in your life. This takes humility. Be open to their response and let God reveal to you any areas where pride has crept in.

Pray About It

Heavenly Father, rid me of any pride. There is no room for pride in my life; search me and address any area in which I am prideful. I want to walk in humility to be closer to You. Help me seek humility and turn from pride. Reveal to me people who are humble so I can follow their lead and be an example of humility. I pray my future husband acts in humility instead of pride. I pray we are selfless toward one another and honor one another. In Jesus's name, Amen.

Today's Scriptures:

God opposes the proud but shows favor to the humble. (James 4:6b)

If I must boast, I will boast of the things that show my weakness. (2 Corinthians 11:30)

Day 5 Reflection Questions

1. How can you show more humility?

\
\
\

2. How does the way you think, speak, and act change when you walk in humility?

\
\

3. Are the people around you prideful or humble?

\
\

4. How do you respond to people who are prideful?

\
\
\

5. Have you seen pride take you down the wrong path?

\
\

Day 6: Pray for Contentment

Contentment. The battle to be content is never-ending. The world tells us that the more you have or the more you do, the more you matter. That's a lie. With God, what we have is a blessing from Him, and the things we do are enough for Him. Our God is a God of simplicity. He knows what we need, exactly when we need it.

Contentment comes from trusting God with the things we already have. It is trusting that God will guide and provide. Let God know that what you have now is enough for you and that He is enough to sustain you. We can have confidence that Christ will provide all our needs. We entered this world with nothing, and we will leave it with nothing.

> But godliness with contentment is great gain. For we brought nothing into this world, and we can take nothing out of it. But if we have food and clothing, we will be content with that. (1 Timothy 6:6-12)

Do you get a thrill when a package arrives at your doorstep? Influencers are constantly reminding us of the things they think we absolutely need because they work so well for them. I sometimes find myself buying something because I am curious to see if I'll have the same results. I want what they have, and it is just as available for me as it is for them. I quickly jump to the conclusion that I should buy what they have. I have done this often. New things are nice, but the intention behind the purchase will help us determine whether we should hit the "Buy Now" button or not. It is easy to make a quick purchase without processing the motive behind it. My guilty pleasures include water bottles, leggings, and lots of Amazon finds. I'll hear that the newest iPhone comes out and try to reason why I need it. Having the most is not the best and does not make me more important. How many of these items do I really need?

Being content is a daily choice. I can be content with what I have and thank God that what I have is enough.

> Do not store up for yourselves treasures on earth, where moths and vermin destroy, and where thieves break in and steal. But store up for yourselves treasures in heaven, where moths and vermin do not destroy, and where thieves do not break in and steal. For where your treasure is, there you heart will be also. (Matthew 6:19-21)

He cares about our accomplishments but is more concerned about our heart.

The way we honor and obey Jesus should be more impressive than the things we own. There will be a day when we will give an account of what we have done for Jesus. What will we tell Him? He cares about our accomplishments but is more concerned about our heart. We are told to store up treasures in heaven, not on earth. We mistake our accomplishments for treasures. When you picture yourself standing before God, what do you have to show Him? What treasures have you stored up in heaven while living on earth? The cell phone, designer purse, overpriced leggings, and sparkly diamond ring will no longer exist. It will be just you and God, so if you want to impress Him, honor Him. Christ is enough. In Him we will find true contentment.

> They are surprised that you do not join them in their reckless, wild living, and they heap abuse on you. But they will have to give account to him who is ready to judge the living and the dead. (1 Peter 4:4-5)

Challenge:

Be mindful of your belongings. Clean out a cluttered space to organize and understand what you have, what you need, and what you can get rid of. Purge! Throw away (or give away) belongings that you no longer use or are unnecessary. They can be as small as hair products or as big as a prom dress. It is a bonus if you can bless someone else with something you already have.

Process your purchases with these questions:

1. Is this a want or a need?

2. How often am I going to use this?

3. Will it benefit or hurt my health?

4. Can I afford this right now?

5. Why do I want to make this purchase?

Make a habit of getting rid of something old every time you get something new (shoes, special skincare products, candles, clothing, whatever). We all have that one item we like to collect and feel we never can get enough of, but truthfully, we may not need it.

Pray About It

Jesus, help me be content with what I have. Help me to be content in this season. Reveal to me what it is like to be truly content in Your eyes and not my own. I want to be content because I trust You, God. I trust that You will provide for me in the areas of my life where I feel like I am searching for more. Quiet the parts of my mind and heart that always want more and more. Today I ask that You sustain me more than anything else. I know a relationship with You is better than anything this world will ever offer me. Make me content and satisfied with the things You have already provided for me. In Jesus's name. Amen.

Today's Scriptures:

But godliness with contentment is great gain. For we brought nothing into this world, and we can take nothing out of it. But if we have food and clothing, we will be content with that. (1 Timothy 6:6-12)

Do not store up for yourselves treasures on earth, where moths and vermin destroy, and where thieves break in and steal. But store up for yourselves treasures in heaven, where moths and vermin do not destroy, and where thieves do not break in and steal. For where your treasure is, there you heart will be also. (Matthew 6:19-21)

They are surprised that you do not join them in their reckless, wild living, and they heap abuse on you. But they will have to give account to him who is ready to judge the living and the dead. (1 Peter 4:4-5)

Day 6 Reflection Questions

1. What are the essentials for you? What do you *need* in order to be content?

____

____

____

2. What do you have that you could do without?

____

____

____

4. What does God say you need in order to have true contentment?

____

____

____

5. Are you focused on treasures on earth or storing up treasures in heaven? What would it look like if you started storing up treasures in heaven? What does that mean?

____

____

____

____

Day 7: Pray He Will Be a Father with Godly Character

Whether you desire to have children or not, a man with the characteristics of a good father should resemble our Father in heaven. Here are a few correlations between our good heavenly Father and a good earthly father. Both are the following:

- **A Protector.** He watches over you and brings a sense of safety to the atmosphere.

- **A Provider.** He satisfies the needs of your family, so you know you can depend on him.

- **A Leader.** He is disciplined and sets a good example, making sacrifices for his family.

- **A Supporter.** He is encouraging, involved, compassionate, and loving.

These qualities are those we should look for in the man who will father our children. You should pray about these attributes and be aware of them as you are in the dating stage of a relationship.

As parents, we will have the power to plant seeds of Scripture and structure into our children. At a young age, they are moldable, curious, and willing to learn. We can guide them and lead them to the Lord by engaging in conversation about Jesus, playing Christian children's music, and practicing prayer before bed, in addition to daily modeling that practice. This structure will help set a solid biblical foundation for their future.

Start children off on the way they should go, and even when they are old they will not turn from it. (Proverbs 22:6)

As Christian parents, it is our responsibility to raise our children in a way that honors God. We are in the process of becoming more spiritually mature ourselves, yet, at the same time, we can bring up our children to live the same way. Let's make heaven crowded! As we become parents, we need to keep in mind that our children are watching our actions and words. What we do can give us a glimpse of who they will become. From a very early age, a child discovers their personality, tendencies, even their own flaws. Set the best example you can. Do it for them, but also for you.

> It is our responsibility to raise our children in a way that honors God.

Children are a heritage from the Lord, offspring a reward from him. Like arrows in the hands of a warrior are children born in one's youth. Blessed is the man whose quiver is full of them. They will not be put to shame when they contend with their opponents in court. (Psalm 127:3-5)

Challenge

Reflect on how you were raised and how you want your children to be raised. You cannot expect your children to attend church if you are not attending church. Find a church that fills your spirit and teaches straight from the Bible. Research churches online and visit their website to learn what they believe. Ask other Christians where they attend.

Pray About It

Heavenly Father, I pray my future husband speaks life and truth into our children and me. I desire for him to be a protector, provider, leader, and supporter for our family. Help us plant seeds about who You are in the lives of our children so they will learn what it's like to have a relationship with You at a young age. Along with that, I pray for our children's children to know You and live for You. Let our family's legacy be one that honors You forever. In Jesus's name. Amen.

Today's Scriptures:

Start children off on the way they should go, and even when they are old they will not turn from it. (Proverbs 22:6)

Children are a heritage from the Lord, offspring a reward from him. Like arrows in the hands of a warrior are children born in one's youth. Blessed is the man whose quiver is full of them. They will not be put to shame when they contend with their opponents in court. (Psalm 127:3-5)

Day 7 Reflection Questions

1. Are you active in a church?

____

2. What do you want your family to value someday?

____

____

3. What do you want your family to prioritize?

____

____

4. Does the man you are currently talking to, dating, or engaged to, have the characteristics outlined above? Does he protect you? Is he a man of godly influence?

____

____

____

5. How is he influencing you? How does he lead you?

____

____

6. Do you have vision of him leading your family towards God?

____

____

Day 8: Pray for His Physical Health

What we buy at the grocery store is what we will eat. If we buy junk food, loaded with sugar, fat, and sodium, and other highly processed products, we are likely to eat it. If we don't buy it, we must put in some extra effort and money to find it. We control what food goes into our bodies.

> Since our body is a temple of the
> Holy Spirit, it should be well-cared
> for and well-nourished.

What are you feeding yourself? And how are you doing it? Taking time to plan healthy snacks and meals requires work. It requires thinking about what to eat, determining if it is healthy, going to the grocery store, putting the groceries away, and then you still have to cook the food! That's a lot of effort, but it is what we must do if we desire to take good care of our bodies. Since our body is a temple of the Holy Spirit, it should be well-cared for and well-nourished.

> Do you not know that your bodies are temples of the Holy Spirit, who is in you, whom you have received from God? You are not your own; you were bought at a price. Therefore honor God with your bodies. (1 Corinthians 6:19-20)

It is easy to eat unhealthy food. It's cheap, convenient, and formulated to appeal to our sense of taste. Sometimes I can eat double the recommended serving size, but what if I chose to eat healthy food instead?

That is something you must really want to make happen. Otherwise it won't. You can only change what your body wants but not what it needs. To choose fruit as a sweet snack over chocolate sounds crazy, but if you train your body to desire healthy foods, it will start to crave them. Making small changes can affect the way you feel. An example is choosing an apple over a baguette at Panera Bread. It's a sacrifice, but a healthy one.

Our bodies go through a lot during our lifetime. I played volleyball in high school and college, and now that I don't play a sport consistently, I need to make sure I am staying active. My body craves it. If you are able, make it a point to be active. I encourage you to make it a priority. That looks different for everyone; it can range from an evening walk to a high intensity interval training class. Do what is best for your body to strengthen it.

Our spirit needs to be fed too! Just as we eat every day to sustain our body, our spirit needs to eat. Jesus told us He is the bread of life. He sustains us. He lives inside of us, and He satisfies us.

> Then Jesus declared, "I am the bread of life. Whoever comes to me will never go hungry, and whoever believes in me will never be thirsty." (John 6:35)

Challenge

Try something new that could benefit your physical health. Here are some suggestions:

- ➤ Go to the gym or invest in a home gym.

- ➤ Try a new fitness class.

- ➤ Set a goal to walk 10,000 steps a day. Your neighborhood is a good place to start.

➤ Keep a food diary for a week, and take stock of what you are eating.

➤ Try meal planning and prepping.

➤ Try intermittent fasting.

➤ Make a list before you go to the grocery store, and make an effort to purchase whole foods.

➤ Research the effects of processed foods on the body.

➤ Drink more water.

Pray About It

Lord, I pray for my future husband's body, that he may be strong and healthy. I pray against disease, aches, and illnesses. I pray healing over pain that may afflict him. Help him recognize the importance of his health and be intentional about taking care of his body. God, may his life honor You with each step and every place he goes. Help us both to crave healthy foods to sustain us. Guide us in living our lives in a way that honors these bodies You created. Thank You for making our bodies a place for Your Holy Spirit to dwell. In Jesus's name. Amen.

Today's Scriptures:

Do you not know that your bodies are temples of the Holy Spirit, who is in you, whom you have received from God? You are not your own; you were bought at a price. Therefore honor God with your bodies. (1 Corinthians 6:19-20)

Then Jesus declared, "I am the bread of life. Whoever comes to me will never go hungry, and whoever believes in me will never be thirsty." (John 6:35)

Day 8 Reflection Questions

1. How can you take better care of your body?

2. Are you nourishing your body with the food you eat?

3. Are you aware of the things you are putting into your body?

4. Are you treating your body as a holy temple?

6. Examine your eating and exercise habits. Are there foods you can sub-stitute or ways you can incorporate exercise into your daily routine? What is the first step you need to take?

Day 9: Pray for Clear and Consistent Communication

Improving communication is an essential part of every relationship. Being able to express our thoughts, feelings, and emotions can be difficult. We want to be effective communicators because our words can be confusing, misinterpreted, and hurtful. Too often, I have spoken quick and angry words, allowing myself to react without thinking about the impact my words might have. Allowing our feelings to speak can cause damage. We need to be cautious of the words we speak because they carry weight. We need to respond and not just react. Words can hurt, and they tend to replay in our mind too. Sometimes you can remember the exact place, atmosphere, and person that spoke them. Let's use our words wisely.

> The tongue has the power of life and death, and those
> who love it will eat its fruit. (Proverbs 18:21)

Our words set us apart and are a reflection of what is going on in our heart and mind. God doesn't want us to gossip, swear, or grumble. Our words should mirror pure intentions and healthy motives. They should be used to empower others because that is what is in our heart to do. Our words should be intelligent, compassionate, and full of thanksgiving because that is what is in our mind. We have allowed words to come out of our mouth without taking our thoughts captive. Think before you speak.

Our words set us apart and are a reflection of what is going on in our heart and mind.

Being a good listener is part of having good communication skills. When you listen, you are empathizing with others and validating their thoughts and feelings. When you listen, you are showing someone else that the attention does not have to be on you. We all want to be heard when we have a point to make. Just being present and listening could be all someone in your life needs. It takes skill to listen and then retain the information and details you've been told. Friends recognize this when you follow up with them about their siblings, a big test they had, or something as simple as how their weekend plans went. Those conversations do not go unnoticed. They say something about who we are. Listening requires us to take the focus off of ourselves and place it on someone else, sending them the message that they are important and you value them. It is trying to understand the other person's perspective. Listen before you respond.

> My dear brothers and sisters, take note of this: Everyone should be quick to listen, slow to speak, and slow to become angry, because human anger does not produce the righteousness that God desires. (James 1:19-20)

The Bible reminds us to be quick to listen and slow to speak. Give yourself grace in the moments in which words have been said but not meant. Be willing to apologize when you say something hurtful. Accept responsibility for the times you respond in anger, and ask God to change that part of you.

Perhaps it is hard for your current boyfriend/fiancé to express his feelings. If so, you need to talk about that. Create a space for him to open up and tell you any concerns that may be on his heart. You don't want to push him to talk about how he feels, but sometimes it's hard for us to talk about our feelings with the people we love most. Be vulnerable with one another about the things God lays on your heart. I promise, God put those things there for a reason. This will cultivate a relationship with depth. You should be able to approach one another without hesitation.

Be sure to pray before those conversations. Ask the Lord—the One who can change the situation—to bring understanding and help to you both, even before you share your thoughts, feelings, or concerns with each other. God can comfort and relieve your worries and cares. The Holy Spirit will give you words to speak and help you use them in a way that pleases Him. That's a much better option than speaking out of your own emotion.

Challenge

Here are some examples of how to communicate your thoughts. Be mindful of how you communicate with someone, so it is done in a way that is both honest and helpful.

Instead of:	Try Saying:
I am not mad *or* you made me mad!	I felt hurt when you said…
Leave me alone *or* "the silent treatment"	I need time to process this. I want to revisit this conversation, but I can't right now.
I am fine.	I feel upset and need some time to gather my thoughts.

Filter out unwholesome talk. We can retrain our minds to use encouraging words instead of discouraging words, complimenting instead of cursing, and praising instead of complaining. Discipline yourself when you speak words that slipped out without restraint. We have the power to control our tongue, and we can choose to repair the breach when we fail.

> Your people will rebuild the ancient ruins and will raise
> up the age-old foundations; you will be called Repairer
> of Broken Walls, Restorer of Streets with Dwellings.
> (Isaiah 58:12)

Pray About It

Heavenly Father, help my future husband and me to have mature and vulnerable conversations about how we feel. Help us to understand the root of our feelings and be able to express them to one another without hurt. Holy Spirit, drive our words, not our emotions. When it comes to tough decisions we make together, let Your voice be louder than any other and help us come into agreement with one another. Let our choices individually and as a couple be God-honoring, not self-honoring. Help my future husband know that he can communicate with me about any topic, good or bad. God, give him the strength to respond with gentleness, kindness, and understanding. In return, help me to respond with patience, love, and compassion. Lord, give us wisdom to communicate effectively and forgive one another in all circumstances. In Jesus's name. Amen.

Today's Scriptures:

My dear brothers and sisters, take note of this: Everyone should be quick to listen, slow to speak, and slow to become angry, because human anger does not produce the righteousness that God desires. (James 1:19-20)

The tongue has the power of life and death, and those who love it will eat its fruit. (Proverbs 18:21)

Your people will rebuild the ancient ruins and will raise up the age-old foundations; you will be called Repairer of Broken Walls, Restorer of Streets with Dwellings. (Isaiah 58:12)

Day 9 Reflection Questions

1. Can you admit that words you speak sometimes come off your tongue differently than you had hoped?

____

____

2. How honest and open do you think you are on a scale from 1-10 with 10 being "very honest" and 1 being "not honest"?

____

3. Are you trustworthy?

____

4. How could listening better impact your future conversations?

____

____

____

5. Take time to reflect on your conversations: Are you doing most of the talking? Or are you being a good listener and retaining the information people tell you?

____

____

____

____

Day 10: Pray He Has a Servant's Heart

Serving is giving without expecting anything in return. Serving is an active form of love and a selfless way to show others that you care and are willing to give without getting. Jesus is the Master Servant. In His life, He found ways to serve others often. He came to earth to serve others, not to be served.

> Each of you should use whatever gift you have received
> to serve others, as faithful stewards of God's grace in its
> various forms. (1 Peter 4:10)

Serving is a sacrifice of time and effort. Instead of cultivating a servant's heart, we often view serving as an inconvenience or less of a priority compared to the other things we need to get done. However, the truth is that our time and efforts are used most efficiently when we are serving others. It would be selfish of us to think otherwise.

If you see a need not being filled,
maybe it is your time to step up and
start something new.

Our generation is known for committing to an action and then never following through with it. We are nonchalant about basic church attendance, and even more so, with serving in the church. The church needs our efforts, not only on Sunday, but throughout the week. There are more than enough opportunities for us to spend time building the kingdom of God. If you see a need not being filled, maybe it is your time to step up and start something new within your church body. The momentum you bring will help propel others. If you say you are going to serve at church, commit and do it. Commit to what you said you would do. Let's change the opinions people have of our generation.

Every day, we are God's servants. We serve God by spending quiet time alone with Him in prayer, reading the Bible, and worshipping him. Jesus was strengthened by prayer and spending time with His Father, and we are too. We need to be better about seeing this as an opportunity to serve our heavenly Father. Let's commit to serving Christ for the rest of our lives.

> Whoever serves me must follow me; and where I am, my servant also will be. My Father will honor the one who serves me. (John 12:26)

Challenge

Offer your time to serve in your community or in your church. This is a great way to meet new people and serve your city well. Ask where help is needed, commit to serving others, and then show up. Go to events, help with setting up and tearing down, or be a greeter! Go where God leads, and let Him use you. You are an expression of His love to the world.

Pray About It

Lord, I pray my future husband and I both have a heart to serve others and You. Plant a strong desire to serve others deep within our hearts. May we be reliable, faithful, and committed to our responsibilities. As a couple, help us demonstrate what it looks like to be dedicated to the church and Your people. Cultivate a servant spirit within us, so we can faithfully serve in Your church. In Jesus's name. Amen.

Today's Scriptures:

Each of you should use whatever gift you have received to serve others, as faithful stewards of God's grace in its various forms. (1 Peter 4:10)

Whoever serves me must follow me; and where I am, my servant also will be. My Father will honor the one who serves me. (John 12:26)

Day 10 Reflection Questions

1. Define what serving means to you.

2. Have you ever noticed how easy it is to serve when you want to? What would happen if you cut something out of your schedule to serve more or if you served in an area that pushed you out of our comfort zone? What would that look like in this season of your life?

3. Are you actively serving at your church? If not, learn what the Bible says about using your gifts to minister to others.

Day 11: Pray for His Confidence

onfidence has peaks and valleys in everyone's lives. It isn't just a struggle for women; men deal with it too.

I lack confidence in public speaking. While I've been told it's a skill I have, I don't see it myself. It's something I'm afraid to do. The talent others see in me, I do not see in myself. I lose confidence just thinking about speaking in front of others. This is the challenge I face when asked to speak. I agree with confidence, and later, deal with my true lack of confidence. Whether it's a presentation in a classroom, work, or to a group of young adults, I always agree to do it. Even though I am uncomfortable and feel inadequate, I agree to it because, with time and practice, I will become confident even in this situation that intimidates me now. I remind myself that I am capable and trust that I will make it through (and it won't be as bad as I imagine!)

> But blessed is the one who trusts in the Lord, whose confidence is in him. (Jeremiah 17:7)

> With time and practice, I will become confident even in this situation that intimidates me now.

We all fall into one of three categories when it comes to self-confidence:

The Confident You: These are the days when you compliment yourself, are satisfied with yourself, hold your head up high, and stand strong in who you were made to be.

The Kinda-Confident You: These are the in-between days where you just coast; your confidence is not running high, but it is not hitting low either.

The Defeated You: These are the days when you feel insecure, incompetent, and inadequate. None of your clothes fit right, someone made an upsetting comment about your life, and you just want to crawl back into bed, throw the covers over your head, and stay there. We've all had those days.

We grow in confidence because the power of Christ dwells within us. If you find your confidence in the Lord, over time you will identify with the Confident You more consistently. You won't have to experience the Kinda-Confident or Defeated You. Speaking the promises of God over your life will help you identify with His voice more than the voices inside your head that try to diminish the truth God speaks about who you are. The caution here is to be able to notice the difference between confidence and arrogance. The Confident You will not boast except in things the Lord has done. Less of you, more of Him.

How do we overcome this turbulent roller coaster of confidence? We do this by combating the lies in our head with the truths God has given us, thereby building our confidence in the Lord. Stand tall, and know that your strength comes from the Lord.

You are perfectly and wonderfully made! You are a daughter of the King! You are a conqueror and an overcomer! Remind yourself of those things daily. I am who God says I am, not the names that have been spoken over my life. I refuse to identify with the labels from my past. The Bible says I am chosen and fashioned for good things, clothed in strength and dignity, and created for a purpose by God. Declare who God says you are over your life. Walk in confidence, knowing that you are a woman of God, and God only has good things to say about you. Your confidence comes from Him alone. In fact, we are going to call it *Godfidence.* This is the name that tops the Confident You, the Kinda-Confident You, and the Defeated You: the Godfident You.

Challenge

Write yourself a letter and include things you like about yourself. Take it even further and write what God says about you as His child.

Detox from social media and identify the changes. See if you do different things or think differently when you are not spending so much time on your phone and no longer subjecting yourself to a forum that makes you constantly compare yourself to others.

Pray About It

Heavenly Father, I admit there are days I struggle with self-confidence. Help me break free of any self-doubt. I know that's not from You. You have called me and chosen me for a purpose. I pray this for my future husband as well. Help him to have full confidence in You and full confidence in who You have created him to be. When we are together, may our words build one another's confidence. Reveal Your promises about who You say we are. Lord, let Your voice be the loudest one in our lives. Give us confidence in ourselves because we have full confidence in You. In Jesus's name. Amen.

Today's Scripture:

But blessed is the one who trusts in the Lord, whose confidence is in him. (Jeremiah 17:7)

Day 11 Reflection Questions

1. What do you like about yourself?

____

____

2. What do you do well? What skills do you possess?

____

____

3. What qualities do others remark upon?

____

____

4. Where do you lack confidence? How can you overcome that area of lack?

____

____

5. What are you doing to gain more confidence?

____

____

6. Is your confidence rooted in Christ? How do you know this?

____

____

Day 12: Pray He Knows How Much He Is Loved

If you don't know God, you won't know true love. God is love. We cannot comprehend the depth of God's love for us. Jesus is waiting with open arms every day. When we are wrapped in His arms, we are in the safest and most secure place we can ever be. We love others because He showed us His love first.

> Dear friends, let us love one another, for love comes from God. Everyone who loves has been born of God and knows God. Whoever does not love does not know God, because God is love. This is how God showed his love among us: He sent his one and only Son into the world that we might live through him. This is love: not that we loved God, but that he loved us and sent his Son as an atoning sacrifice for our sins. Dear friends, since God so loved us, we also ought to love one another. No one has ever seen God; but if we love one another, God lives in us and his love is made complete in us. (1 John 4:7-12)

The Greek language uses four different words to describe love, while English only has one word for it. We see these in the Bible: *eros, storge, phileo,* and *agape.* Let's take a closer look at them to better understand them and to help us identify the different loves we experience throughout our lifetime.

Eros is the romantic love between a man and a woman. It's a longing and willingness to do anything or go anywhere just to be with them. This love also covers sexual attractiveness and the desire to be with someone intimately. Jacob worked seven years on Rachel's father's farm and then, after being deceived, another seven years until he could finally be with the one he loved. Song of Solomon contains the most intimate portrait of this love found anywhere in the Bible.

Storge is the love between family members. This is the way parents, children, and siblings love each other. Esther and Mordecai were cousins. They were loyal and faithful to one another (and God) in a time when they could have been killed for their Jewish faith.

Phileo refers to brotherly love. This is the love we have for friends and those we care for and want to have as part of our life. This describes the deep bond between brothers and sisters in Christ—the community of believers with whom we interact on a regular basis. The disciples were a group of acquaintances that had one common goal (following Jesus). They had their moments of strife but grew to travel and work together.

Agape is the unconditional love God has for us. Jesus's death on the cross powerfully demonstrated that love. He loved us so much that He was willing to suffer and die for our sins. This love is willing to lay down a life to show others the way.

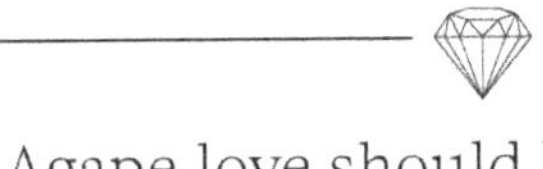

All four of these are crucial for our experience. However, agape love should be the focus of our life. God's love is greater than the love of man, and it is the only type of love that will sustain us eternally. Agape love will never leave us feeling forsaken or forgotten.

I pray that out of his glorious riches he may strengthen you with power through his Spirit in your inner being, so that Christ may dwell in your hearts through faith. And I pray that you, being rooted and established in love, may have power, together with all the Lord's holy people, to grasp how wide and long and high and deep the love of Christ, and to know this love surpasses knowledge—that you may be filled to the measure of all the fullness of God. (Ephesians 3:16-19)

Challenge

Write a letter to your future husband. Let him know how loved He is by our heavenly Father and how you will love him someday. Tuck it somewhere safe to share with him at the right time in the future.

Read today's verses more than once and in multiple versions. Read them out loud, slowly, and meditate on the power of the words. Let this be our mindset today and every day.

Pray About It

Jesus, fill my life and surround me with Your love. It is my hope that my future husband feels your agape love so strongly today that he can't help but talk of the love You have for him. I pray that he feels incredibly loved and adored by You. Let Your love be the center of our lives. Let all that we do flow from a place of love because You loved us first. Thank You for Your love that surpasses all understanding. In Jesus's name. Amen.

Today's Scriptures:

Dear friends, let us love one another, for love comes from God. Everyone who loves has been born of God and knows God. Whoever does not love does not know God, because God is love. This is how God showed his love among us: He sent his one and only Son into the world that we might live through him. This is love: not that we loved God, but that he loved us and sent his Son as an atoning sacrifice for our sins. Dear friends, since

God so loved us, we also ought to love one another. No one has ever seen God; but if we love one another, God lives in us and his love is made complete in us. (1 John 4:7-12)

I pray that out of his glorious riches he may strengthen you with power through his Spirit in your inner being, so that Christ may dwell in your hearts through faith. And I pray that you, being rooted and established in love, may have power, together with all the Lord's holy people, to grasp how wide and long and high and deep the love of Christ, and to know this love surpasses knowledge—that you may be filled to the measure of all the fullness of God. (Ephesians 3:16-19)

Day 12 Reflection Questions

1. Evaluate yourself, and recognize what type of love you spend your time focusing on and seeking out.

____

____

____

____

2. Can you identify these four types of love in your life?

____

____

____

____

3. What kind of love do you recognize most in your life? Which is the most important to you?

____

____

____

____

____

Day 13: Pray for His Mental Health

Have you ever tried to process the thousands of thoughts racing through your brain daily? Does even considering this cause your thoughts to spiral out of control even more than they already are? If we focus on the things God tells us to focus on, our thoughts will become more guided as we allow Him to direct them. Philippians 4:8-9 tells us to think about the things that are true, noble, right, pure, lovely, admirable, excellent, and praiseworthy. The good news is that Jesus is all of these things! Our thoughts should center on Christ. Only He can change the way we think. You have the power to control your thoughts, but your thoughts will lean toward righteousness when you surrender that power and ask God to govern your mind.

> Finally, brothers and sisters, whatever is true, whatever is noble, whatever is right, whatever is pure, whatever is lovely, whatever is admirable—if anything is excellent or praiseworthy— think about such things. Whatever you have learned or received or heard from me, or seen in me—put into practice. And the God of peace will be with you. (Philippians 4:8-9)

There are neural pathways in our brain which send signals from one part of the brain to the other.[1] If the same thought takes the same route repeatedly, it becomes a habit. Our goal is to know the root behind the habits of our brain. We need to better understand why we think the way we do. Once we get to a place where we understand our own mental pathways, we will be able to better understand ourselves.

---

1. Grace Weintrob, "How to Rewire Your Brain," Center for Healthy Aging, May 31, 2022, https://www.research.colostate.edu/healthyagingcenter/2022/05/31/how-to-rewire-your-brain/

Set your minds on things above, not on earthy things. (Colossians 3:2)

> We need to better understand why we think the way we do.

Do you not like your current thought patterns? Does the past sneak in and sabotage your day? To begin, let's change our mindset about counseling. There's a line of thought prevailing in the church that only weak people seek counseling. That is not true. We are not perfect; everyone has things wrong with them. There are things wrong in our brain. Some thoughts make it to our brain without us understanding the *why* behind them. Sometimes we need help from someone who is trained to help us dig into the root of a thought issue.

Do not conform to the pattern of this world, but be transformed by the renewing of your mind. Then you will be able to test and approve what God's will is—his good, pleasing and perfect will. (Romans 12:2)

The experiences we have had in the past are real, and they have shaped us. They need to be worked through properly. We can only go so long until we recognize how great our need is for a healthy brain. Counseling can teach us how to manage our thought processes and give us the tools we need to cope when we feel overwhelmed or anxious. Your brain is a vital part of your body and sometimes needs a doctor. Your brain needs care and correction too. Therefore, it needs just as much attention as you give to the chiropractor for your back or the optometrist for your eyes.

Challenge

Take some time to pause and reflect on your thoughts. Journal your thoughts, anxieties, fears, and frustrations. This can be a therapeutic tool you may have never utilized before. Surround yourself with people with positive growth mentalities. Talk to a trusted friend or an older and wiser godly woman in your church. Ask more questions. You can find real growth in asking the question: *Why*? If you feel you need to go deeper, research Christian counseling in your area.

Pray About It

Lord, I pray for Your protection over my future husband's mind. Shield him from the lies of the Enemy. Help him to clearly discern between Your voice and any other. Give him strength to resist the lies of the Enemy and only choose the truth about the man You say he is. I pray he will not entertain confusion but live in clarity. He will not be tormented with impure, evil, negative, or sinful thoughts; he will be transformed by the renewing of his mind. Help him to see that You are the focal point in his life. Together we want our thoughts to be guided and understood. In Jesus's name. Amen.

Today's Scriptures:

Finally, brothers and sisters, whatever is true, whatever is noble, whatever is right, whatever is pure, whatever is lovely, whatever is admirable—if anything is excellent or praiseworthy— think about such things. Whatever you have learned or received or heard from me, or seen in me—put into practice. And the God of peace will be with you. (Philippians 4:8-9)

Set your minds on things above, not on earthy things. (Colossians 3:2)

Do not conform to the pattern of this world, but be transformed by the renewing of your mind. Then you will be able to test and approve what God's will is—his good, pleasing and perfect will. (Romans 12:2)

Day 13 Reflection Questions

Ask yourself these questions:

1. Do I think through my choices before acting on my thoughts?

____

2. How have past experiences shaped the way I think now?

____

____

3. How is the condition of my mind? Do my thoughts ever take over in a damaging way?

____

____

4. What is my mind focused on?

____

____

5. Do I need to talk to someone about my thoughts, struggles, or feelings?

____

6. Do I have fears about asking for help?

____

____

____

Day 14: Pray for His Family and Extended Family

Marriage unites two people, but it also unites two families. That can be overwhelming but also a blessing. Pray that your future husband's family treats you with love and respect, and in return, that you will reciprocate that same love and respect to them. Pray for a genuine connection and strong, healthy relationships for your husband with his family as well as with your family. Pray for them even if you don't know them yet.

> A friend loves at all times, and a brother is born for a time of adversity. (Proverbs 17:17)

This is what family is. Family are the people we lean on when times get tough. Pray that he has a family that supports you and encourages you when there are trials. Pray for his family to encourage you in your walk with the Lord. In those challenging seasons of life, pray that you are guided by family members who are leading you to God-honoring decisions.

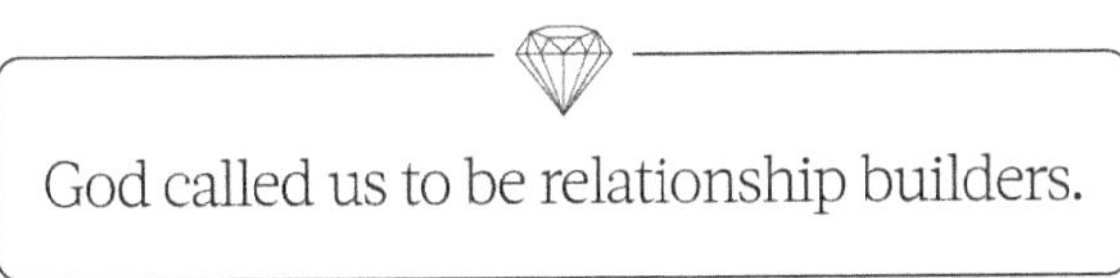

God called us to be relationship builders.

We should also be praying for family members who have not accepted Jesus Christ into their life yet. I encourage you today to continually fight for their salvation in daily prayer. Let your actions of love and consistent prayer be an example of Christ. Allow God's love to be so evident in your life that they can't deny the love they feel when they are around you. Help others find their way by having faith for them, and hope that they will be drawn to know Him too. We believe they will find Jesus.

God called us to be *relationship builders*. That does not mean we need to strive to be liked. Instead, we must live in peace with all people—family, friends, coworkers, colleagues, and so on. If you haven't made things right with your siblings or parents, have a conversation, forgive them, and do whatever you need to do to be right with them again. Do this for yourself, and work to come into a place of peace with them. Let them know that the past is past, and the new has come. Strive to make things right again. Breakthrough in the lives of your loved ones is possible.

> If it is possible, as far as it depends on you, live at peace
> with everyone. (Romans 12:18)

We can start today by praying for our future husband's health, safety, and protection. Disease, sickness, and pain are evident in our world, but every day, we need to be reminded that the God we serve is a God that loves, forgives, and heals. He makes things new again. We can do the same.

Challenge

Invest in time with your family by showing up to family events, sharing good memories, or playing games. Enjoy quality time with your family now. You will have your own someday! Have open, honest, vulnerable conversations with family members you have hurt—or who have hurt you—as led by the Lord.

Pray About It

Heavenly Father, Thank You for the gift of family. Thank You for the people You have placed in my life to call family. I am waiting in eager anticipation to meet my future husband and start a new family with him. I am excited to meet his family and have new family members to call my own. I lift up the family members that have not come to know You. I pray they experience You and choose to live their life for You. I pray against every disease and sickness that may try to come against my current family and my future family. Please protect us in all we do. In Jesus's name. Amen.

Today's Scriptures:

A friend loves at all times, and a brother is born for a time of adversity. (Proverbs 17:17)

If it is possible, as far as it depends on you, live at peace with everyone. (Romans 12:18)

Day 14 Reflection Questions

1. How are you preparing now for your future family? What habits can you cultivate now to benefit your future family?

____

____

____

____

2. What do you want the core beliefs of your future family to be someday?

____

____

____

3. When you think of your future family, what do you see? What vision do you have for your future family?

____

____

____

5. Who are you feeling led to pray for in your family? What specific area can you be praying for them about? Invite the Lord into it.

____

____

____

Day 15: Pray He Finds Hope in His Heavenly Father

Just because you haven't met your future husband yet, while your friends are already getting married or having children, don't lose hope. If it has been three years since you have been on a date, don't lose hope. Even though you went through a really tough breakup and it seems like there is never going to be anyone for you again, don't lose hope. Be encouraged. It will happen.

> Now faith is confidence in what we hope for and assurance about what we do not see. (Hebrews 11:1)

Most often, we have to wait for what God has promised. Hope is the anticipation within us while we wait. People break promises and disappoint us time and time again, but God is true to His Word *all the time*. He is faithful in the waiting. We can trust that what He says will happen. We need to have hope like an anchor, firm and secure. God's promises will not be broken.

> We have this hope as an anchor for the soul, firm and secure. (Hebrews 6:19a)

Women of faith, hope for things not yet seen! Just because it hasn't happened yet doesn't mean it won't. Understand that there is a purpose for why God hasn't given us what we desire, even if we don't understand why right now. Choose to have faith and believe for the things God will do. Hope brings anticipation and can propel us to action. Hope can be the very thing that leads you to opening your own business, believing for healing, or seeing the unsaved find salvation.

I once told a friend that "everything can change in six months." She replied, "Anything can change in one month!" Our lives can drastically change for better or worse in just minutes, days, or hours. Even in the bad, we have an opportunity to hope for good. Through Jesus, hope can be injected into any hopeless situation. Cling to hope. One moment with the Lord can change everything.

> Just because it hasn't happened yet
> doesn't mean it won't.

Jesus is our hope. We live in a fallen, broken, and imperfect world. How wonderful that we can find hope in Jesus Christ! He is the hope of the world because He is the only One who can save. Believe for a man whose hope is in Jesus Christ and His promises. We are waiting for a man who is willing to wait for God's promises and possesses wild hope in a world that says there is none. He is worth the wait.

Challenge

Make a list of the things you hope will happen in the next year, and another for the next five years, and tuck them away. Continue to hope until you sense it is time to revisit your list again.

Look at promises found in the Bible and write down the ones you sense God is speaking to you. When you feel your hope is lost or slipping away, speak nothing but what God has promised over your life.

Pray About It

Lord, help me to have unshakable hope in who You are. Spark my vision for the future, and fill it with expectation of what You can do. As for my future husband, give him hope in the mo-

ments that seem discouraging and difficult. I pray that he finds hope in what may seem like a hopeless situation. Together we want to look to You as the Source of our hope for the days ahead. In Jesus's name. Amen.

Today's Scriptures:

We have this hope as an anchor for the soul, firm and secure. (Hebrews 6:19a)

Now faith is confidence in what we hope for and assurance about what we do not see. (Hebrews 11:1)

Day 15 Reflection Questions

1. What are you hoping for most right now?

____

____

____

____

2. What seems hopeless? How do you overcome you own lack of hope?

____

____

____

____

3. How can you increase hope in your life?

____

____

____

____

4. Who are you hoping for, and what are you hoping for them?

____

____

____

Day 16: Pray He Lives a Life of Purity

God did not design us to be with more than one partner. His plan is for each of us to be joined together with one partner for a lifetime. Abstaining before marriage isn't a restriction, it is for our protection. Ask God for conviction about this. His forgiveness and grace will cover the things you may have already done and give you an opportunity to live in purity again. Grace, however, does not allow us to keep doing what we once did.

> Flee from sexual immorality. All other sins a person commits are outside the body, but whoever sins sexually, sins against their own body. (1 Corinthians 6:18)

Did you read that? *Flee* from sexual immorality. Turn and run! If you don't, it will chase you down and capture you. This verse says you are sinning against yourself when you do this outside the covenant of marriage. You are working against yourself when you stay in temptation and fall into sexual sin. We were made for a covenant relationship: a commitment we make to one another that cannot be broken. Traditionally, wedding ceremonies take place in a church where you commit to the person you have chosen, in the presence of God and your family and friends. When you get married, you make a commitment to someone that should never be broken; it is locked, sealed, and fastened for life.

What does God say about sex? It is good, but it was designed for marriage. When you get married, you leave your father and mother and start a new family with your spouse. Marriage is a commitment to one another—the two become one flesh. Until that point, we are to protect ourselves and abstain from dishonoring God. If you are not being obedient, you are being disobedient. It's that clear.

> We were made for a covenant relationship: a commitment we make to one another that cannot be broken.

But at the beginning of creation God "made them male and female." "For this reason a mean will leave his father and mother and be united to his wife, and the two will become one flesh. So they are no longer two, but one flesh. Therefore what God has joined together, let no one separate. (Mark 10:6-8)

How can we live a life of purity? It begins with surrendering to God. Commit to wanting to stay pure. Your partner must want that too. Otherwise we may find ourselves doing something we know is wrong. Set specific boundaries. Avoid too much time alone or hanging out past a certain time at night. Agree together that the motive behind physically touching each other must remain pure and is not to be sexualized. Draw the line and do not cross it. That will help you avoid sin. We can't be putting ourselves in situations that could lead to sin. If we are walking toward sin, we are bound to step into it. If we turn and walk away from sin, we are less likely to do it. Setting boundaries with your partner will protect you both. Having others hold you accountable will hold you to the commitments you have made.

How can a young person stay on the path of purity? By living according to your word. I seek you with all my heart; do not let me stray from your commands. (Psalm 119:9-10)

Challenge

Make a decision to live in purity from this moment forward. Choose to set boundaries. Be intentional with where you go, who you are with, and what you do together.

Pray About It

Lord, purify me of any sexual desire that is dishonoring to You. Position me in a way to understand the effects of sex outside of marriage and the joy of sex within marriage. Today I am making a commitment to You and my future spouse to honor You with my body. I pray my relationship is pure and strengthened by Your Word to do what is right in Your eyes. In Jesus's name. Amen.

Today's Scriptures:

Flee from sexual immorality. All other sins a person commits are outside the body, but whoever sins sexually, sins against their own body. (1 Corinthians 6:18)

But at the beginning of creation God "made them male and female." "For this reason a mean will leave his father and mother and be united to his wife, and the two will become one flesh. So they are no longer two, but one flesh. Therefore what God has joined together, let no one separate. (Mark 10:6-8)

How can a young person stay on the path of purity? By living according to your word. I seek you with all my heart; do not let me stray from your commands. (Psalm 119:9-10)

Day 16 Reflection Questions

1. Do you understand the importance of why God made sex for *after* marriage?

____

____

2. If yes, why is that important to you personally?

____

____

3. If no, how can you gain insight into God's plan for you so you understand this better?

____

____

4. Have you ever asked God to help keep you pure?

____

5. What specific boundaries can you set to live a life of purity?

____

____

6. Are there any areas of your life in which you feel you are walking in sin? What would help you turn and walk in the opposite direction?

____

____

Day 17: Pray He Is a Good Steward Financially

There is a multitude of references to money in the Bible and how to use it. God wants to be a part of our finances. He knows our financial situation better than we do. He knows where we stand financially now and in the future. Let's break down how to live financially by using three G's: gaining, greed, and giving.

> For the love of money is a root of all kinds of evil. Some people, eager for money, have wandered from their faith and pierced themselves with many griefs. (1 Timothy 6:10)

Gaining

A common misconception is that money gives you power. With Jesus, the opposite is true. Jesus gives us a spiritual power, and money is meaningless. Jesus wants us to be honest, truthful, and patient when it comes to our finances. We need to be good stewards of how we spend our money, making thoughtful and intentional decisions with what God has provided.

If we can't live without it, we are living for it.

> Dishonest money dwindles away, but whoever gathers money little by little makes it grow. (Proverbs 13:11)

Note the consequence for dishonesty and the reward for saving (or gathering) money. Growth comes when we save.

Greed

We tend to hold money with a strong grip. I've learned that holding onto something too tightly—maybe a past relationship, a car, clothing, or even social media—can indicate that it's becoming an idol. An idol is anything we allow to come before God. If we can't live without it, we are living for it. If you find yourself trying to justify why you need it, there is a good chance you don't. If we can't let it go, it must go. God can rid us of idolatry if we allow Him to do that.

> Whoever loves money never has enough; whoever loves wealth is never satisfied with their income. This too is meaningless. (Ecclesiastes 5:10)

Giving

Be a cheerful giver. Bless others with your finances. Receiving isn't the hard part. Giving is. Have you ever thought, *If I made more, I would give more?* I used to think that until I recognized that what I have now is enough to give. I can give more if I focus on what I have less. This is a true act of selflessness and an area in which you can never be too obedient. If God is over all, He is over your finances as well. Be generous.

> Each of you should give what you have decided in your heart to give, not reluctantly or under compulsion, for God loves a cheerful giver. (2 Corinthians 9:7)

Challenge

Cut one area of spending out of your week. Maybe it is a coffee, a pair of shoes, or eating out. Evaluate if what you are spending your money on is necessary or not. Can you do without it? Pray about how you use your money.

Practice generosity by tithing to your local church. Tithing is giving a portion of what we were given to the church. We do this because what we make belongs to the Lord. We are to steward it well.

Pray About It

Heavenly Father, as I pray for my future husband today, I pray that he works hard to gather his money and that he is wise with what he spends it on. I pray he understands how to steward finances well. As a couple, may our understanding of finances be based on biblical truths. I pray that together we can make financial decisions that are honoring to You. If there are any idols or traces of greed in our hearts today, I ask that You remove them. In Jesus's name. Amen.

Today's Scriptures:

For the love of money is a root of all kinds of evil. Some people, eager for money, have wandered from their faith and pierced themselves with many griefs. (1 Timothy 6:10)

Dishonest money dwindles away, but whoever gathers money little by little makes it grow. (Proverbs 13:11)

Whoever loves money never has enough; whoever loves wealth is never satisfied with their income. This too is meaningless. (Ecclesiastes 5:10)

Each of you should give what you have decided in your heart to give, not reluctantly or under compulsion, for God loves a cheerful giver. (2 Corinthians 9:7)

Day 17 Reflection Questions

1. How can you be a good steward of your finances?

____

____

2. Is there anything in your possession that you are holding onto that you just can't let go?

____

____

3. Is there anything you don't want to share? What are you holding onto selfishly?

____

____

4. Are you tithing regularly?

____

5. Are you honoring God with your finances? If not, how can you do this better?

____

____

6. Are you able to recognize any idols in your life?

____

____

Day 18: Pray That His Passions, Callings, and Gifts Are Revealed to Him

When we receive a gift, it is meant to be used. God did not give us talents, skills, and abilities so we would place them on a shelf. They are meant to be used for His good. We can sharpen and enhance our God-given gifts daily.

If you don't know what your spiritual gifts are, make a list of areas you naturally excel at, as well as those areas in which people have complimented you. Ask a well-trusted friend or family member to help you identify your gifts. Another way to discover this part of yourself is by determining what you are passionate about. What are you excited to learn about? You know you are passionate about something if you are eager to learn more about it.

We learn about spiritual gifts in Romans and then again in 1 Corinthians:

> We have different gifts, according to the grace given to each of us. If your gift is prophesying, then prophesy in accordance with your faith; if it is serving, then serve; if it is teaching, then teach; if it is to encourage, then give encouragement; if it is giving, then give generously; if it is to lead, then do it diligently; if it is to show mercy, do it cheerfully. (Romans 12:6-8)

➢ Romans names prophecy, serving, teaching, encouragement, giving, leading, and mercy as gifts from God.

To one there is given through the Spirit a message of wisdom, to another a message of knowledge by means of the same Spirit, to another faith by the same Spirit, to another gifts of healing by that one Spirit, to another miraculous powers, to another prophecy, to another distinguishing between spirits, to another speaking in different kinds of tongues. All these are the work of one and the same Spirit, and he distributes them to each one, just as he determines. (1 Corinthians 12:8-11)

➢ First Corinthians adds words of wisdom, words of knowledge, faith, healing, miraculous powers, prophecy, discerning of spirits, speaking in tongues, and the interpretation of tongues to that list.

We are to use our gifts and not be jealous of the gifts others have. Focus on the things you are capable of and grow in your gifts. First Corinthians 12:6 says, "There are different kinds of working, but in all of them and in everyone it is the same God at work." Whoa! Let's just take a moment to think about that today. This is saying there are different kinds of gifts and talents in people, but the same God gave them to everyone. God made each of us with cool talents, including you. God is all-knowing. He knows what we need to succeed. There is a reason He did not give you the same talents someone else has. Each of us is unique. He has given you specific talents on purpose. The same God that created you also created me and is at work in different ways inside each of us.

Position yourself in a place where you just want to be where God called you to be.

God gives us mentors to help grow the potential that is inside of us. They challenge us with questions we dread like, "What are you called to do?" I always feel like my answer is not good enough because I am still trying to figure out what God has appointed me to do. What I do know is that I desire to be where God has called me, and I will keep taking steps forward into the places He is guiding me. Maybe you know your calling and are walking that out, or maybe you are still trying to navigate it. Position yourself in a place where you just want to be where God called you to be. He will guide, direct, and lead you if you are submitted to Him. Let Christ reveal the calling He has placed on your life; in the meantime, listen and obey.

Challenge

As you seek the Lord, He will reveal your giftings. Ask the Lord to help you discover the purpose for your life. Get to know God better by asking Him, "What are You calling me to do?" "What have You created me to do?" "Where do You want to send me, God?" Ask Him to reveal where you should be. Seek mentorship so you can be sharpened and challenged by someone who has achieved things you desire to achieve someday.

Pray About It

Heavenly Father, today I pray You use my talents to honor You. May my future husband and I develop our God-given purpose. Show us the things You have called us to do. I pray that whatever we do in this life, we would be a reflection of who You are. Spark passion in us so we can be used for Your good. Thank You for creating us with gifts and abilities that are unique, and help us to use our lives for Your glory. In Jesus's name. Amen.

Today's Scriptures:

We have different gifts, according to the grace given to each of us. If your gift is prophesying, then prophesy in accordance with your faith; if it is serving, then serve;

if it is teaching, then teach; if it is to encourage, then give encouragement; if it is giving, then give generously; if it is to lead, then do it diligently; if it is to show mercy, do it cheerfully. (Romans 12:6-8)

To one there is given through the Spirit a message of wisdom, to another a message of knowledge by means of the same Spirit, to another faith by the same Spirit, to another gifts of healing by that one Spirit, to another miraculous powers, to another prophecy, to another distinguishing between spirits, to another speaking in different kinds of tongues. All these are the work of one and the same Spirit, and he distributes them to each one, just as he determines. (1 Corinthians 12:8-11)

Day 18 Reflection Questions

1. What do you get excited about doing?

____

____

2. What sparks passion inside of you?

____

____

3. What could you spend hours on and never get tired of doing?

____

4. In what areas of your life have you seen your gifts in motion?

____

5. What gifts have you been given?

____

____

6. What careers, hobbies, or qualities do not sound appealing to you? (To learn about your gifts and abilities, you may need to determine what they are not.)

____

____

____

Day 19: Pray He Is a Man of Prayer

It's important to remember the impact of prayer in your relationship. No prayer is wasted; your heavenly Father hears *all* prayer. Everything you speak to God is heard. In the midst of hard seasons, when He may seem quiet, He is still listening. Be bold in going to Christ in every struggle, challenge, and battle. Christ fights your battles for you. We need to be fighting our battles in the Spirit before we can truly battle them in life.

> This is the confidence we have in approaching God: that if we ask anything according to his will, he hears us. (1 John 5:14)

A man of God speaks to the Lord every day. We hope he is praying blessings over our future relationship and family already. We hope he is bold when he talks with God and declares things over his life. We hope he will be comfortable praying with his friends and family. We hope he is able to discern a situation and ask, "Can I pray with you?" Or say, "Let's pray about it," in excitement to talk to God. As a couple, we want to make time to spend in prayer over our meals, our careers, our family, and beyond.

Christ fights your battles for you.

Prayer shows our trust in God. It opens a door to give God access to our heart. As we bring our cares and lay them at His feet, we believe our prayers will bring transformation through the power of the Holy Spirit. Only He can change our circumstances. In the simplest way, prayer is a conversation with God. All relationships begin with getting to know one another through conversation. Avoid limiting prayer to church or a quick uttering of thanks when you're about to eat. Since our prayers are heard 24/7, we can pray 24/7. We can talk to Him in the car, at work, while grocery shopping, or at home. Wherever we are, He is with us. Invite Him into your every moment.

> Where can I go from your Spirit? Where can I flee from your presence? If I rise on the wings of the dawn, if I settle on the far side of the sea, even there your hand will guide me, your right hand will hold me fast. (Psalm 139:7-10)

Here are a few things I've incorporated that have helped my prayer life:

- Pray a verse or chapter from the Bible over your life. (Jesus modeled this for us.)

- **P.U.S.H.**: **P**ray **U**ntil **S**omething **H**appens!

- Stay focused on *Who* you are speaking to when you pray.

- Pray specific and bold prayers.

- End with "In Jesus's name" because there is power in the name of Jesus.

- Give thanks. There is always something to be grateful for every day.

Challenge

A prayer journal is an excellent way to track our prayers and the answers God provides. Write down what you are praying and believing for every day. This encourages us to believe for big things and keeps a record of God's faithfulness.

Set reminders to spend time in prayer.

Pray out loud. It may be uncomfortable at first, but it is better to speak it out rather than bottling it up inside. There is power in the words you speak. Each morning, start with a simple prayer thanking Him for the new day. Pray that you draw closer to Him. Try acknowledging God with a "good morning" *before* you acknowledge social media. Giving God the first five to fifteen minutes of your day can change the outcome of the rest of it. You are setting yourself up for a good day when you start it with God on your mind.

Pray About It

Lord, thank You for giving me a voice. I want to use it to speak to You daily. I know You hear my prayers, no matter where I am. Holy Spirit, be welcomed into every prayer I speak. Increase my knowledge of prayer, and help me to communicate better with You every single day. I pray my future husband is a man of prayer and lays his cares at Your feet. Guide us to pray bold powerful prayers. In Jesus's name. Amen.

Today's Scriptures:

This is the confidence we have in approaching God: that if we ask anything according to his will, he hears us. (1 John 5:14)

Where can I go from your Spirit? Where can I flee from your presence? If I go up to the heavens, you are there; if I make my bed in the depths, you are there. If I rise on the wings of the dawn, if I settle on the far side of the sea, even there your hand will guide me, your right hand will hold me fast. (Psalm 139:7-10)

Day 19 Reflection Questions

1. Do you pray bold prayers?

____

2. Do you fully believe God hears your prayers? Or is there hesitation?

____

____

3. What does your prayer life look like?

____

____

4. How much time do you spend in communication with God? How much is He on your mind?

____

____

5. Are you nervous about praying out loud? How can you overcome that fear?

____

____

6. How can you incorporate prayer throughout your day?

____

____

Day 20: Pray for Healing from Past Relationships

The heart-wrenching pain of a breakup is not an experience we want to go through. It might feel easier when we are the one breaking up with the guy, but when he is the one doing the breaking, it really hurts and doesn't seem fair. If you haven't experienced that yet, be grateful and continue to guard your heart. If you have experienced heartbreak, I ache with you but want you to know that God is near. In those moments when our heart sinks and sorrow sets in, we are vulnerable to the temptation of seeking fulfillment somewhere else. Good news, friend, the Lord is close to the brokenhearted. That emptiness you feel can be relieved by Jesus.

> The Lord is close to the brokenhearted and saves those
> who are crushed in spirit. (Psalm 34:18)

If we discuss a breakup, we also need to look at the post-breakup. While in a relationship, we are invested emotionally, spiritually, mentally, and sometimes physically. When it ends, we can be damaged in all of those areas, carrying the weight of the baggage that occurred during the relationship. This can include disappointment over broken promises, shame over unhealthy boundaries, and even abuse. Sometimes we come out of a relationship unrecognizable to who we once were. It happens. There is grace to cover it, but the healing process must begin. We were not made to jump from one relationship to the next. We must heal from the past hurt. Otherwise, we will carry that hurt into our next relationship. It would not be fair to our future husband if we entered a relationship with him while still thinking about a previous love. That is a sign you are not ready to be in a relationship again.

We cannot stack one painful relationship on the next without giving attention to what is underneath. We want to be whole and free from the past or we will take that brokenness into the next season. It is a process, but if we lay it at the feet of Jesus, He will walk with us through it. He will guide us into the healing our heart longs for. Start with confessing the areas where you have been wrong and done wrong. Repent and turn from the way you once were. Ask Jesus for forgiveness and to make you whole again. Through the power of the Holy Spirit, your broken heart can be restored! Break free from past hurt and walk in freedom. You can't stay in that place any longer. It's time to move on and move closer to the Lord.

> Therefore, if anyone is in Christ, the new creation has come:
> The old has gone, the new is here! (2 Corinthians 5:17)

> We cannot stack one painful relationship on the next without giving attention to what is underneath.

Challenge

Forgive the person who hurt you. Do not dwell on past relationships. Don't forget, but don't obsess on what once was. Address your hurt. Resist any urge to hang out somewhere he might show up. Don't text him out of a lonely state of mind or ask others about him if it still hurts you. Establish healthy boundaries with him and mutual friends.

If necessary, seek help via a counselor or pastor for spiritual guidance on healing and wholeness.

Pray About It

Lord, I come to You today asking for complete healing from past relationships. Forgive me. I recognize that only You can fill me, so please, God, come do what You do best. I want to be whole and healed when I meet my future husband someday. I ask these same things for my future husband too. I pray that he has called on You to fill every part of his heart that has been bruised or broken in the past. When we come together, I hope we both have hearts that are whole and ready to be shared with one another. I pray for Your healing hand on our lives. I pray we both break free from chains that have kept us bound. Help us walk in Your freedom. In Jesus's name. Amen.

Today's Scriptures:

The Lord is close to the brokenhearted and saves those who are crushed in spirit. (Psalm 34:18)

Therefore, if anyone is in Christ, the new creation has come: The old has gone, the new is here! (2 Corinthians 5:17)

Day 20 Reflection Questions

1. Do you often think about someone with whom you were in a past relationship? How frequently? Are you healed from your past relationship(s)? How do you know?

____

____

____

____

____

2. Do you want to break free from the past? What is the first step you need to take?

____

____

____

____

3. Do you need to forgive someone or yourself from the past? What is the best way to do that?

____

____

____

____

Day 21: Pray He Is Zealous to Share the Truth of the Gospel

This prayer is for everyone who wants to live for Jesus. We can all be bold in sharing the truth of Jesus Christ. As Christians, our mission is to share the love of Jesus by living according to His Word and making disciples.

> He said to them, "Go into all the world and preach the gospel to all creation." (Mark 16:15)

Gospel means *good news*. There is no better news than the truth that Jesus Christ died on the cross and three days later came to life again. He rose again, saving us from our sin and creating a gateway for us to live eternally with Him. We pray to invite the Holy Spirit into our life and ask for forgiveness from the God who saves our soul. This is when repentance takes place. We leave behind who we once were and walk into a new life by inviting Jesus into our heart. From this moment on, we seek God and let Him transform us. He will move us in ways and put us in places we never imagined. When you invite Jesus into your life, your spirit is awakened. Be aware that the devil will try to deceive you to keep you in the place you used to be, but with the Holy Spirit's power living inside of you, the devil will not be able to succeed.

Sharing the gospel is not to be taken lightly. We must discern the right moment, so we will know when to speak and when to wait for the right opportunity. We must allow the Holy Spirit to bring us into situations in which we can share our testimonies of His goodness and faithfulness in our lives. This is our chance to share God's love with others. We have an opportunity to do this daily. Wisdom teaches us to discern when to share with someone. People are generally more receptive to someone they know and have developed a relationship with, rather than someone who just starts trumpeting a sermon. Use the relationships you already have as a place to start sharing the love of Christ. These people are already watching the way you act and listening to how you speak. Your influence comes over time, and along with that come depth and trust. Look for ways to share what God has done in your life, and leave a space for them to respond.

> Use the relationships you already
> have as a place to start sharing the
> love of Christ.

When people see the things God has done in your life, they may start to wonder what that would look like in theirs. Your story tells of the power of Jesus. It shows that you were once one way, but through Jesus, you are made new.

> For I am not ashamed of the gospel, because it is the power of God that brings salvation to everyone who believes: first to the Jew, then to the Gentile. (Romans 1:16)

We are all called to share the gospel. Not one person is excused from that calling, as God has placed it on us. If we are carriers of *good news,* we must get excited about it. It's hard to withhold information you are excited to share with others. When it comes to sharing the gospel, look for a man who is fearless in his pursuit to tell others about who Jesus is and what He has done.

Challenge

Dive deeper into the Gospels: Matthew, Mark, Luke, and John. They are filled with rich truth and the story of Jesus dying on the cross, taking our sin, and rising again.

- Talk with one person about Jesus this week.

- Ask God for an opportunity and the boldness to share the gospel with someone.

- Write out your testimony. Share your testimony and ask others about theirs.

Pray About It

Heavenly Father, I pray my future husband has the boldness to share the gospel. Reveal to him a greater knowledge and understanding about what the gospel means, and give him boldness to share it with others. Bring us opportunities to share the gospel. As we tell others about You, give us discernment for how to approach conversations that put You in the center. Empower us to be unashamed of the gospel, and help us share Your story more frequently. In Jesus's name. Amen.

Today's Scriptures:

He said to them, "Go into all the world and preach the gospel to all creation." (Mark 16:15)

For I am not ashamed of the gospel, because it is the power of God that brings salvation to everyone who believes: first to the Jew, then to the Gentile. (Romans 1:16)

Day 21 Reflection Questions

1. Have you ever shared the gospel with anyone before? How can you
   set yourself up to tell others about Christ?

2. Have you ever shared your testimony?

3. Do you allow Jesus to be the center of your conversations? Do you
   pray about conversations before you go into them? Ask the Holy Spirit
   to guide you in these moments.

Day 22: Pray for Him to Cultivate Patience

Patience is a fruit of the Spirit—one not easily obtained. If you struggle with being patient, you are not alone. Keep pursuing it, but know that it is built through tests. Learning to wait is hard. Practice waiting while shopping, ordering food, and with your friends and siblings. We could all use more patience.

Our lives are fast-paced, and we keep adding more and more to them because we want to accomplish so much. I have found that the days go by fast when I have everything planned and get myself fully booked. Our culture tells us to live this fast-paced lifestyle, assuring us that if we do more, we will achieve more. If we always have plans, we must be important. Unfortunately, we pack our schedules so full that we often have an excuse to say we don't have time to do the most important things—the things that really matter—like eating home-cooked meals, spending quiet time with the Lord, visiting our parents, or going for a walk.

When was the last time we slowed down? The slowing of our activities, schedules, and plans leads to a life of patience. If we don't always have something to do next, we start to grasp what it really means to turn down the fast pace and reset.

> A man of patience is a blessing
> from God.

A man of patience is a blessing from God. Can you picture the way he will be with you if he has patience? He will be slow to become angry when you are not having a good day or are in a bad mood. Can you imagine what it will be like when you parent together? A patient man won't be easily frustrated. He will take time to invest in your children, and he will teach them to be patient instead of demanding. He will speak gently instead of harshly. Patience is a skill that requires you to stop, think, and then respond.

> A hot-tempered person stirs up conflict, but the one who is patient calms a quarrel. (Proverbs 15:18)

If you look at the life of Jesus, you will see that He was never in a hurry, so we don't need to be either. Slow down, girl! We are in a season of waiting for our future husband, so let's practice patience. The truth is that we will need patience very often in our life since everything is not available to us as soon as we want it. This is the perfect time to slow down, unwind, and be renewed. Since we are in a season of preparation, we do not have any other option than to be patient. Let's use our time wisely and settle into this season of patience as we let God teach us a lesson.

> But if we hope for what we do not yet have, we wait for it patiently. (Romans 8:25)

Challenge

Time management is being mindful of how we spend our time and how much we invest in certain tasks. Take a break from your cell phone or social media. Note how you spend your time when you are not mindlessly scrolling. Set parameters for yourself. Go on a device-fast for a certain number of days, or set screen-time restrictions in order to create better habits. The goal is to make room in your life for what is most important.

Here are some things we can do while we wait: worship, journal, read, seek God, find community, invest in others, and spend time in prayer.

Pray About It

Lord, today I ask for an abundance of patience for my future husband. Help him to endure any chaotic moments with peace and perseverance. I also pray for patience in my own life. Allow me to use this season to its fullest by being patient in the plans You have for my future. Guide me to be more poised and collected in the trying moments. Together, help us understand the importance of a slow-paced and peaceful lifestyle that is not always chasing after the next thing. In Jesus's name. Amen.

Today's Scriptures:

A hot-tempered person stirs up conflict, but the one who is patient calms a quarrel. (Proverbs 15:18)

But if we hope for what we do not yet have, we wait for it patiently. (Romans 8:25)

Day 22 Reflection Questions

1. How can you strengthen your patience?

____

____

2. How can you slow down your current schedule?

____

____

3. Are you able to recognize the moments you are least impatient?

____

4. Examine yourself to recognize your level of need for something to go faster than it currently does. What is causing you to live a fast-paced lifestyle? Why do you think that is?

____

____

5. What do you focus on the most? What do you spend the most time doing?

____

____

6. What is the outcome of where you spend your time? Are you being intentional with your time?

____

____

Day 23: Pray He Is a Man of Honor and Respect

Recently, a couple I know was asked when they were getting a new dog. They both answered at once. He said, "In a few years." She said, "By the end of summer." Their conflicting responses provide a good illustration about being able to find a resolution to a problem. One option might be compromising by meeting halfway with a time frame that works for both. Another option would be to put the other person's desire first and honor what they want more than what you want.

The Bible is clear about how a wife is to submit to her husband as the head of the household. By design, God made the man the one who represents the household. He is the gatekeeper through which everything must pass to get into that home. As women, we are the partner that stands next to him and supports him. A husband and wife must constantly work together, not against each other. The more you agree on parenting, in-laws, family, and finances, the more you continue to build. Wives should be able to trust that their husbands are going to make the best choices for their home and the people they love.

> A husband and wife must constantly work together, not against each other.

Ephesians 5 outlines how the church submits to Christ. We are the church that is meant to be submitted to the Lord. One line of what is quoted below reads: "Husbands, love your wives, just as Christ loved the church."

Just as a husband desires to be with his wife, God desires to be with us. Imagine a groom on his wedding day: He is standing and waiting for his bride to walk down the aisle. His desire is to enter into a union with her, a lifelong one, which is "till death do us part." As believers, we are already a bride! We are the bride of Christ—the church. Jesus is the Bridegroom, and He is waiting for us to commit to Him as we live our earthly lives, knowing we will be with Him forever. Husbands must love their wives the same way that Christ loves us.

> Wives, submit yourselves to your own husbands as you do to the Lord. For the husband is the head of the wife as Christ is the head of the church, his body, of which he is the Savior. Now as the church submits to Christ, so also wives should submit to their husbands in everything. Husbands, love your wives, just as Christ loved the church and gave himself up for her to make her holy, cleansing her by the washing with water through the word, and to present her to himself as a radiant church, without stain or wrinkle or any other blemish, but holy and blameless. In the same way, husbands ought to love their wives as their own bodies. He who loves his wife loves himself. (Ephesians 5:22-28)

In a relationship, we should be respectful when we talk to, and about, each other. We should be mindful of one another's boundaries and privacy. The man should treat the woman in a way that shows deep love and admiration. The way he acts and speaks about you shows whether he respects you or not.

> Husbands, in the same way be considerate as you live with your wives, and treat them with respect as the weaker partner and as heirs with you of the gracious gift of life, so that nothing will hinder your prayers. (1 Peter 3:7)

Challenge

Develop consistent respect. Respect looks different in each relationship you have. You may have more respect for your parents than you do for your younger siblings. When you first meet someone, you want to make a good first impression. Make eye contact, listen carefully, and ask questions to get to know them more. What if we respected our family in the same way we do someone we just met? What would that look like?

Honor your pastors, professors, teachers, parents, mentors, grandparents, and managers this week in a way that makes them feel like they are important to you. Thank them, serve them, and show them how valuable they are to you.

Pray About It

Heavenly Father, I desire to be married to a man who respects me and continually acknowledges my concerns. I pray his actions represent respect and that he honors others well too. Allow him to consider my opinions and validate them when they are right and redirect me when I am wrong. I pray for a man who will encourage me and help me see my way through every struggle I may face. Lead him to make the best decisions for our home. Help me to submit to him throughout our lifetime together. In Jesus's name. Amen.

Today's Scriptures:

Wives, submit yourselves to your own husbands as you do to the Lord. For the husband is the head of the wife as Christ is the head of the church, his body, of which he is the Savior. Now as the church submits to Christ, so also wives should submit to their husbands in everything. Husbands, love your wives, just as Christ loved the church and gave himself up for her to make her holy, cleansing her by the washing with water through the word, and to present her to himself as a radiant church, without stain or wrinkle or any other blemish, but holy and blameless. In the same way, husbands ought to love their wives as their own bodies. He who loves his wife loves himself. (Ephesians 5:22-28)

Husbands, in the same way be considerate as you live with your wives, and treat them with respect as the weaker partner and as heirs with you of the gracious gift of life, so that nothing will hinder your prayers. (1 Peter 3:7)

Day 23 Reflection Questions

1. What does respect look like in a relationship?

____

____

____

2. How do you show someone you respect them?

____

____

3. How do you hope to make others feel during conversations?

____

____

____

4. Are you lacking in respect for people in your life?

____

____

5. How do you honor others well?

____

____

____

If you are in a relationship:

1. Do you feel heard and seen?

2. Are you trusting each other? Or is there a lack of honesty?

3. Are you communicating thoughts and feelings well with one another?

4. Are you encouraging one another? Or competing?

5. Are you accepting one another's differences? Or disagreeing?

Day 24: Pray He Will Have the Courage to Approach You at Any Time

What do you think it would be like to approach you from a man's point of view? He may be intimidated, shy, or nervous around a strong and confident girl.

Have I not commanded you? Be strong and courageous.
Do not be afraid; do not be discouraged, for the Lord your
God will be with you wherever you go. (Joshua 1:9)

Initiating a conversation can be awkward for anyone. Acknowledge him for showing interest in you. He might be fearing rejection and rehearsing what to say. Give him some grace. It takes courage to approach you! If the man God has for you hasn't approached you yet, pray and believe that he will. If you've already encountered the man you hope to marry, thank God every day.

Guard your heart from situations, people, and emotions that try to steal your peace.

Be on your guard; stand firm in faith; be courageous; be strong. (1 Corinthians 16:13)

Let's break this verse apart piece by piece:

➢ **Be on your guard:** Be cautious! Guard your heart from situations, people, and emotions that try to steal your peace. Protect yourself from hurt by not oversharing; not everyone needs to know the deepest parts of you. Protect yourself from unrealistic expectations, and refuse to allow circumstances to rule over you.

- ➤ **Stand firm in faith:** When you stand firm, you don't let anything shake you, break you, or tear you down. Stand on the Word of God, and stand on the truths of Jesus Christ. Let Christ be your rock that cannot be moved. He is solid, fixed, and relentless.

- ➤ **Be courageous:** Do not waver or be afraid. Do not fear failure; live fearlessly. Be willing to say yes to God when He asks you to do something greater than you think you can do. He makes us bold and gives us the courage we need for any task He gives us.

- ➤ **Be strong:** To build strength, you need to be able to withstand a great amount of weight. That weight is different for each of us, but how we resist the weight determines our strength.

Perhaps we are the ones who need to take courage and finally respond to, or acknowledge, a Christian man who has been trying to get our attention. We need to be approachable if we are praying to be approached!

Challenge

Build up the courage to do something that is out of your comfort zone, like going to the gym or acting on your dream of starting your own business. Maybe you want to travel by yourself, host a small group, submit your art, or play guitar again—this is your opportunity!

Pray About It

Lord, strengthen me to be the woman of God You've called me to be, and raise up my future husband with Your strength. Let us encourage one another to never be afraid or discouraged, as it says in Joshua. Remind us that You are always with us.

Give my future husband the courage to approach me at the very beginning of our relationship and through the many years ahead. Help me to be available to talk, so he feels he can approach me in any situation. Help him to be bold when it comes to pursuing You and pursuing me. In Jesus's name. Amen.

Today's Scriptures:

Have I not commanded you? Be strong and courageous. Do not be afraid; do not be discouraged, for the Lord your God will be with you wherever you go. (Joshua 1:9)

Be on your guard; stand firm in faith; be courageous; be strong. (1 Corinthians 16:13)

Day 24 Reflection Questions

1. Define courage.

2. How can you develop more courage?

3. How can you show courage today?

4. What is something that takes a lot of courage for you to do?

5. Who do you think is courageous? What actions make them seem courageous to you?

Day 25: Pray He Will Resist Temptation

This topic is something we should be praying for regularly throughout our lives. There will always be temptations, but it's how we respond to them that matters. This sets the course for our life. Temptation presents us with a choice. Either we go after whatever entices us or we flee from it. Saying no is one of the most powerful responses we could ever employ. Saying no is not always the easy choice, especially when what is tempting us is in an area in which we struggle. Saying no is powerful and difficult, but it has a lifelong impact. It may be uncomfortable in the moment, but the outcome of turning away from temptation will always be more fulfilling than giving in to it.

> No temptation has overtaken you except what is common to mankind. And God is faithful; he will not let you be tempted beyond what you can bear. But when you are tempted, he will also provide a way out so that you can endure it. (1 Corinthians 10:13)

Temptation presents us with a choice.

As women, we have a responsibility to not be a temptation to the men in our life. While we can't control what others think of us, we can limit inappropriate thoughts to some extent. Let's pray daily that we carry ourselves as daughters of the King. We were not meant to fit into the crowd. We don't have to dress and act like everyone else. We are uniquely made by God, and our intentions are revealed in the way we act, dress, and speak around men. We have the power to control the way we display ourselves. You can express yourself and dress with style and modesty without compromising. Walk in a way that is trustworthy, not tempting.

In the TV show, *One Tree Hill*, one of the main characters, Brooke Davis, is known for her physical beauty, something she banked on in high school. Brooke has the hair, the style, and the body, and she uses it. She went on to build a successful clothing company called Clothes Over Bros. One of the men who was interested in her on the show asked, "What's under all the clothes, Brooke Davis?" He wanted to look deeper into who she was, instead of just seeing her body and the fame she'd garnered from being a clothing designer. He knew there was more inside of her, and he wanted to know her on a deeper level. He recognized that her heart and identity were greater than anything she could flaunt externally.

Jesus looks at the heart. He wants to know the interior way more than the exterior. Our physical bodies hold together the greatness inside of us. We are not merely humans with a spirit that lives inside of us; we are spirits with physical bodies. Let's honor God with our bodies and be a reflection of what God wants to see. The more you desire Jesus, the more your desires shift.

> But the Lord said to Samuel, "Do not consider his appearance or his height, for I have rejected him. The Lord does not look at the things people look at. People look at outward appearance, but the Lord looks at the heart." (1 Samuel 16:7)

Sexual temptation is just one example. Temptation is broad and can bleed into a multitude of different struggles, such as gambling, shopping, alcohol, gossip, and gluttony, just to name a few. They can be enticing but need to be recognized and fought off. First Corinthians 10:13 says that God will provide a way out in the midst of our fleshly cravings. We are seeking men who know their weaknesses and turn to Jesus when temptation comes their way.

Challenge

Set yourself apart from others by the way you dress. Influence others to walk in modesty, and represent yourself in a way that honors God. If you question why modesty is important to God, do your own biblical research and pray through it. Let God reveal a dress code. Be you, and do it in a way that pleases the Lord.

Seek out an accountability partner with whom you can share your struggles. Ask them to check in with you periodically about temptation. This is a great step if you truly want to turn away from the things that tempt you most.

Pray About It

Dear heavenly Father, with Your power I can resist temptation, and I pray my future husband will too. I pray against the past and present temptations with which we battle. In the future, help us to turn and go in the opposite direction when temptation comes. Holy Spirit, overwhelm us in those moments, and remind us that You have better plans for us than any temptation can offer. I pray that we resist every impure motive and that we distance ourselves from places and people that try to trip us up. I pray that we will not let the devil have a foothold in us. I want to honor You with the way I carry myself. God, I pray that my life will honor You in all I do. In Jesus's name. Amen.

Today's Scriptures:

But the Lord said to Samuel, "Do not consider his appearance or his height, for I have rejected him. The Lord does not look at the things people look at. People look at outward appearance, but the Lord looks at the heart." (1 Samuel 16:7)

No temptation has overtaken you except what is common to mankind. And God is faithful; he will not let you be tempted beyond what you can bear. But when you are tempted, he will also provide a way out so that you can endure it. (1 Corinthians 10:13)

Day 25 Reflection Questions

1. Are you walking with the crowd or against it?

____

2. What is your motive behind what you do and say around men? Does it please God?

____

____

3. What is your motivation behind what you wear? What does your style say about you? How do you want to represent yourself?

____

____

4. What is your focus? Is it your inward beauty or your outward appearance?

____

____

5. Are you able to identify the things that tempt you? Have you said no to your temptations in the past? How can you refuse temptation better?

____

____

6. What active steps can you take to cease unhealthy temptations?

____

____

Day 26: Pray That His Dependence and Trust Is in Jesus Alone

We are adopted into God's family when we believe and accept Jesus as our Lord and Savior. As our Father, God wants what is best for us, and that includes our relationships. Surrendering to God allows Him space to position our heart in the way He wants it. God will reveal and redirect you if you are with someone you shouldn't be with. He'll give you peace and assurance if you are supposed to be with the person you are currently in a relationship with.

> Trust in the Lord with all your heart and lean not on your
> own understanding; in all your ways submit to him, and
> he will make your paths straight. (Proverbs 3:5-6)

This verse applies to us today. I challenge you today to put your trust in the plans God has for you. Surrender your need-to-know mindset, and avoid arguing with God about what's best. His way is the best. Give it to God. This is a weight that is not meant to be carried by you. When you find yourself falling back into the need-to-know, refuse those thoughts and remind yourself that God has a good plan for your life. Trusting means being okay with not knowing the answer. Faith affords us the security of being able to trust. Have faith in God. He will take care of the future. He has been faithful to you so far, and He will continue to do the same. Be okay with not knowing what is next.

Trusting means being okay with not
knowing the answer.

Trusting in what we cannot see is not always easy, but it builds faith. Our actions should reflect the Word of God. This verse reminds us to deny ourselves, our desires, and our plans, in order to fully trust Him. Speak this verse over your life when you doubt God's plans.

> Now faith is confidence in what we hope for and assurance about what we do not see. (Hebrews 11:1)

You are worthy of a God-fearing man who puts Christ first. Trust that at the right time, you will meet the man God is preparing for you. Until then, allow the Holy Spirit to develop you while you wait. In His perfect timing, God will bring you the man who sees your potential and calls out the things he knows you are capable of accomplishing. God will bring the two of you together when you are both ready. Depend on His divine timing. He promises to work all things together for those who love Him and are called according to His purpose.

> God will bring the two of you together when you are both ready. Depend on His divine timing.

> And we know that in all things God works for the good of those who love him, who have been called according to his purpose. (Romans 8:28)

Challenge

Memorize Proverbs 3:5, Hebrews 11:1, and Romans 8:28. Use these verses as tools to remind you of His ways. Bible memorization is essential to our Christian walk and helps strengthen us when we are weak. Process and journal what makes these verses special to you.

Ask God to reveal His plans for you, and then trust that He will answer. The answer may not come right now, but it will come. Be willing to wait.

Pray About It

Lord, I choose to trust You today as I wait for my future husband. I know Your timing is perfect, and I will continue to trust Your ways and not my own. Help me to submit to You. I surrender my plans to You today. Lord, let Your will be done in my life. And for my future husband, I pray that he puts his trust in You in this waiting season. Strengthen his trust in You as we wait in anticipation of meeting each other. In Jesus's name. Amen.

Today's Scriptures:

Trust in the Lord with all your heart and lean not on your own understanding; in all your ways submit to him, and he will make your paths straight. (Proverbs 3:5-6)

Now faith is confidence in what we hope for and assurance about what we do not see. (Hebrews 11:1)

And we know that in all things God works for the good of those who love him, who have been called according to his purpose. (Romans 8:28)

Day 26 Reflection Questions

What does the path you are on right now look like? Is it crooked, rocky, bumpy, blurred? Ask Jesus to reveal the straight path—a path where trusting Him brings you clarity, peace, and stability. What do you want to be? (Highlight or circle one for each below.)

Fully dependent on Christ *or* clinging to your own plans?

Submitted to Christ *or* leaning on your own understanding?

Trusting that God is working all things for good *or* forcing things to look good in your life?

Believing in faith *or* trying to figure it out yourself?

Day 27: Pray for His Career and the Role He Plays Among His Coworkers

No matter what profession our future husband is in, it is essential for him to be an example of Christ, just like it is for us. Perhaps he will be a doctor who gets paid well, a mechanic who comes home with greasy pants and hands, a businessman in a suit and tie, or even a writer working from coffee shops while sipping on lattes all day. To some extent, we have all dreamt of what our husband might be doing. Whatever we see him doing may not be what he really wants, and it is not our job to figure it out for him. We want to see him in a role in which his skills are being used to their fullest—one that is fulfilling to him. We can't get caught up in what he does, but we can get caught up in how God can use him in his role.

We are called to be the hands and feet of Jesus. Though it often feels like we are the hands and feet of our bosses because they call the shots, it goes much deeper with Jesus. Whether we are walking into a classroom, office, a patient's room, or another place altogether, we should be illuminated with the light of Jesus. A season that may seem insignificant to you may have a major impact on the plans God has for your future. The experience you are gaining is not wasted; there is purpose in what you are learning. God will never leave you in a wasted season. When motherhood arrives, let us not forget that we were made to take care of the household and use it to glorify the Lord.

> In the same way, let your light shine before others, that
> they may see your good deeds and glorify your Father
> in heaven. (Matthew 5:16)

If you are in a season in which you are trying to determine what career path to take, remember that you are not tied to just one thing.

Just because you have a degree in a specific field does not mean you must spend the rest of your life doing that. For example, a degree in elementary education does not mean you'll be teaching for a long span of your lifetime. That knowledge and experience can be used in many other ways too. It may take years for you to use your degree. Take a deep breath and release the tension of feeling like your degree runs you. You were made for more than your level of schooling. If you don't have a degree, recognize you are capable without it.

> The experience you are gaining is not wasted; there is purpose in what you are learning.

Take the pressure off of yourself. When you find the line of work you are supposed to do, be grateful and work at it with all your might. God gave you multiple passions, so go ahead and seek new opportunities and explore new roles. Our passions can direct us, but Jesus wants us to follow His lead. It may take time and patience to sift through our passions and find what we are to focus on first. Remember to be patient. God will sort it out in time.

> Whatever your hand finds to do, do it with all your might. (Ecclesiastes 9:10a)

Vocation refers to "a special urge, inclination, or predisposition to a particular calling or career, especially a religious one."[2] In light of that, we should desire two things: A career that honors God, and to be in the place God sees us as best suited. We pray He will reveal that to us. We desire to not just be in a job; we desire to be in our vocation!

---

2. "Vocation," The Free Dictionary, accessed July 7, 2023, https://www.thefreedictionary.com/.

We can show others we are different by how eager we work. We are to work hard as we work for the Lord. The roles we are placed in can be difficult and trying, but working diligently and to the best of our ability is what pleases the Lord. At the end of the day, ask yourself, "Did I do my best today?" If not, give yourself some grace. His mercies are new every morning. If you did your best, it is enough. God will bless your work.

Challenge

Depending on your career, this challenge could look different for you.

- Go above and beyond what is asked of you.

- Assist a coworker by offering to take over some of their tasks or provide them support. Be willing to offer your time to help others.

- Organize or clean out an area of your workspace to help declutter that area.

- Clean up the coffee area that has been a mess for a long time.

- Ask your manager or your boss what you can do to excel in your position.

- Bless a coworker by bringing them coffee or lunch.

Pray About It

God, I come to You in prayer today about my future spouse's career. Lord, I pray he is a hard worker in all that he does. I pray that whatever his hands find, he works at it with all his might. Give him motivation to do all things to the best of his ability. Your Word says we can do all things through the One who gives us strength. Give my future husband strength to do all things through Your power. As we work, may we be an example of Christ to those around us. In our workplace, in school, and at home, let our light shine before others, so they may see our good deeds and glorify You. Help us to be leaders that guide others to You. I surrender my career to You today. In Jesus's name. Amen.

Today's Scriptures:

Whatever your hand finds to do, do it with all your might. (Ecclesiastes 9:10a)

In the same way, let your light shine before others, that they may see your good deeds and glorify your Father in heaven. (Matthew 5:16)

Day 27 Reflection Questions

1. Are you working diligently, or are you just doing enough to get by?

2. If you don't like your current job, are you still working hard at it?

3. Are you a good steward of what you currently have?

4. How can you go above and beyond in your workplace to enhance the atmosphere?

5. Do you know your vocation? What steps can you take to better understand what your vocation entails?

Day 28: Pray for His Heart

We've already discussed the positioning of our heart over the last several days, but there is more. Our heart is powerful, but Jesus is our heart monitor. He knows what makes it flutter and what makes it sink. When it comes to our future husband, God knows what our heart desires. He knows what our heart needs more than we do. We don't always understand what our heart craves, but if we take delight in the Lord, He will satisfy us. The things we want so desperately may not be what God desires for us. If you want what God's heart desires, your relationship with Him will flourish. Our heart's posture needs to be open to accept and receive the love of Christ. A heart needs to be softened before it can become transformed.

> Take delight in the Lord, and he will give you the desires of your heart. (Psalm 37:4)

We need to know how people receive love. I have excitedly hugged friends when greeting them to later learn they do not like physical touch. Awkward. They returned my hug because it was the normal way to respond to close friends in our culture. I've learned that I need to show my affection for them in a different way. While I like greeting friends with a hug, I need to understand that they may not receive love the same way I do. We need to be mindful of how others feel loved and make an effort to give love in the way they receive it.

> Neither height nor depth, nor anything else in all creation, will be able to separate us from the love of God that is in Christ Jesus our Lord. (Romans 8:39)

The love Jesus has for us surpasses all others. No matter your situation, Jesus loves you, and nothing will stop His love. Above all, we need to know this love first. We need to long to know Him with our whole heart. God's love is steadfast; it never ends, and there is always more. Love others the way Jesus loves you. The more you let His love fill you, the more you can overflow with love for others. Our heart was made to love another, and the best way to do that is to learn from the God who loves us the most.

> The more you let His love fill you,
> the more you can overflow with
> love for others.

We will have a lifetime to learn our future husband's heart, but before that, we need to draw near to the heart of God. God's love teaches us how to love. We will love each other better if we go directly to the Source of love. Allow Jesus to wrap you in His arms today. Let the Holy Spirit love you and reveal to you the greatest love ever.

Challenge

Learn how your closest friends and family members receive love, so you can show them you love them in the way they receive it best. This could be through spoken words, one-on-one time together, gifts, buying flowers, doing dishes or errands, or a hug. Be intentional in the way you love others.

Close your eyes and visualize what your relationship with Jesus looks like. Picture yourself in a room with Him. What do you see? Does He seem far off, or do you go running to fall into His arms? Ask Christ to wrap you in His arms today, so you will feel comforted, secure, and loved by Him. Ask God to show you His love. You will never get enough, and it will never run out.

Pray About It

Heavenly Father, thank You for the way You love me. Thank You for the way You have represented love by dying on the cross for me. Thank You for the different ways we are to love one another. Help me to love others well and show that love more often. I pray for the way my future husband receives and shows love. I am excited to learn his heart and be able to intentionally show him love in that way. I pray we complement each other, even if opposites, and that we learn to grow together. Continually reveal to us how loved we are by You. In Jesus's name. Amen.

Today's Scriptures:

Take delight in the Lord, and he will give you the desires of your heart. (Psalm 37:4)

Neither height nor depth, nor anything else in all creation, will be able to separate us from the love of God that is in Christ Jesus our Lord. (Romans 8:39)

Day 28 Reflection Questions

1. Have you experienced the power of God's love in your life?

____

____

____

2. What makes you feel loved by others?

____

____

____

3. How do you express your love to others?

____

____

____

4. When was the last time you were intentional about asking a friend what makes them feel loved?

____

____

____

Day 29: Pray That You and Your Future Husband Will Break Generational Curses

God created and chose the family you are in. We did not have a choice as to our family, ethnicity, or gender. As children, our important decisions were made for us. Even spiritually, we went to the church our parents attended, if they went at all. We were not asked what we believed or what church we wanted to attend. At such a young age, it may have been hard to know.

> So God created mankind in his own image, in the image of God he created them; male and female he created them. (Genesis 1:27)

The life you've been given has seen trials and challenges. We can't change the past, the environment we grew up in, the food we ate, and the experiences we had. You may have witnessed addiction, depression, suicidal thoughts, anxiety, or other issues that are plaguing our generation. Our past experiences may be affecting us now, but they can be changed for the future. We are so much more than what we're born into. Yes, our parents made us, and we carry their genetic heritage; but as the Holy Spirit molds and mends our lives, everything changes. You can do things in your family that nobody has ever done before. You can change the course of your family's future generations. Through the power of the Holy Spirit, your children do not have to struggle with the same things you have struggled with. Be different from those before you because you are unique. You are more than what people have said about your family, and you have more to give than you know. Break free from what was. Say goodbye to the past and hello to the future. Jesus changes everything!

Yet you ask, "Why does the son not share the guilt of his father?" Since the son has done what is just and right and has been careful to keep all my decrees, he will surely live. The one who sins is the one who will die. The child will not share the guilt of the parent, nor will the parent share the guilt of the child. The righteousness of the righteous will be credited to them, and the wickedness of the wicked will be charged against them. (Ezekiel 18:19-20)

You have more to give than you know.

Challenge

Ask your grandparents and parents about your family's origin and the tendencies you have, good or bad. Get a better understanding of who you came from, but don't dwell on it. Recognize it and reform it. How do you reform it? Break the cycle.

Pray About It

Heavenly Father, I ask to be freed from any chains holding me from my future. Release perceptions about who I am based on where I came from. Thank You for this life You have given me. Use me in mighty ways. Shift my mentality, change my focus, and make me new in You. Allow me to do things that have never been done before. Use my future husband and I to break every generational curse in both of our families. In Jesus's name, Amen.

Today's Scriptures:

So God created mankind in his own image, in the image of God he created them; male and female he created them. (Genesis 1:27)

Yet you ask, "Why does the son not share the guilt of his father?" Since the son has done what is just and right and has been careful to keep all my decrees, he will surely live. The one who sins is the one who will die. The child will not share the guilt of the parent, nor will the parent share the guilt of the child. The righteousness of the righteous will be credited to them, and the wickedness of the wicked will be charged against them. (Ezekiel 18:19-20)

Day 29 Reflection Questions

1. What changes can you make in your generation?

2. Have you already broken generational curses in your life?

3. What are the healthy characteristics and traits that you will continue to carry on?

Day 30: Pray That He Recognizes His Blessings

"Count your blessings. Name them one by one." Do you recognize that hymn? I remember singing it in church as a little girl. Acknowledging your blessings gives you a glimpse of the goodness of God. We often find ourselves pointing out the negative and dwelling on the worst possible outcomes ahead, but those worst-case scenarios are not from God. We wonder why our current situation is happening, and we are unable to comprehend situations that are beyond what we know. The truth is that all the circumstances we have been stressing about, weeping over, and overthinking have already been taken care of by God. He's got it all worked out. All we have to do is obey. Blessing will follow obedience.

> All these blessings will come on you and accompany you if you obey the Lord your God. (Deuteronomy 28:2)

Some seasons are abundant in blessings, and others feel like living in a desert. Sometimes we feel like we are on the outside watching everyone else receive blessings. We run to God when things aren't working out the way we want or when trauma strikes, or when we find ourselves in the valley. These trying seasons can lead us to the Lord as we ask Him for miracles. When things are out of control, our sense of dependence on Him is greater, but where is He when we are basking in blessings? He is right there with us then too. We shouldn't call on God in the bad moments and leave Him out of the good ones. He is the One who is consistent when we are not. We need to depend on Him during the highs and the lows. When we are living in the blessings, we must thank Him for them.

If you are single, dating, or engaged, continue to count your blessings. A relationship is a blessing, but it is not what we are living for. A relationship is not the end goal. We are living to bless the Lord. If we use this season to search and long for something we think we should have, we will miss it. Our focus is God first.

> The Lord bless you, and keep you; the Lord make his face shine on you and be gracious to you; the Lord turn his face toward you and give you peace. (Numbers 6:24-26)

Challenge

Bless someone else with an act of kindness today. Become a blessing to others. Change up your regular routine that is focused on you, and be a blessing to someone else.

Make a list of things God has blessed you with throughout your lifetime.

Pray About It

Lord, I pray that You use me in a way that I am a blessing to those around me. Please reveal new opportunities to be a blessing. Help me to recognize the ways You have already blessed me. I want to count my blessings daily and always remember to be thankful for the things I have. I pray for my future husband and the blessing he will be to me. I pray for a man who is going to be a blessing to all those around him. In Jesus's name. Amen.

Today's Scriptures:

All these blessings will come on you and accompany you if you obey the Lord your God. (Deuteronomy 28:2)

The Lord bless you, and keep you; the Lord make his face shine on you and be gracious to you; the Lord turn his face toward you and give you peace. (Numbers 6:24-26)

Day 30 Reflection Questions

1. How can you be a blessing to those around you?

2. When was the last time you thanked God for the most important things in your life—like the food you eat, your car, your best friend, your sibling, your parents, your job, and so on?

3. Do you count your blessings on a regular basis? How can you incorporate gratitude into your every day?

A Note from the Author

Dear Reader,

Seek the Lord first in your relationship. We want God to approve of our choice in marriage. He wants to see our relationships thrive now and forever. Pray for discernment as you get to know men. Ask God to remove anything or anyone that is not from Him. If there is a man in your life that shouldn't be there, walk away from that relationship. The Lord will guide you if you are fully surrendered and your heart desires more of Him. Lay everything down at the feet of Jesus. God has something better for you than you can ever imagine on your own.

Wait for the man that will walk with you, guide you, and lead you to a more abundant relationship with Christ. Once you meet him, I hope you choose him every single day for the rest of your life.

Ladies, we are the helpers that are to come alongside a man. We are to help one another through this life together. We need each other; we are a team put together to work together.

> The Lord God said, "It is not good for the man to be alone.
> I will make a helper suitable for him." (Genesis 2:18)

As you close this devotional, I hope you have recognized applicable ways to seek Jesus every day. I pray you desire to know Him with a fiery passion. I pray you crave spending time with Him, and that you have made a commitment to live your life for Him. I pray you make commitments to God first and then the man you choose to marry. I pray you get married and live victoriously, allowing the Holy Spirit to move and have His way in your marriage and in your life. In faith, you have believed for something that has not yet come to pass. When the right man comes, you will be able to say, "I prayed for him!" Your prayers have been heard.

In Him,

Vee Summer

About the Author

Vee Summer grew up in a small town outside of State College, Pennsylvania. Vee is a graduate of Penn State University where she studied Marketing, Management, and Entrepreneurship while playing collegiate level volleyball. Vee spends her time at local coffee shops, working out at the gym, and getting involved with her church community. She is passionate about young adults discovering their identity in Christ, and she desires to empower others to live confidently in relationship with Jesus. In college, she started writing this devotional to encourage herself to pray for her future husband. She then started sharing a condensed version of it with college friends through a thirty-day text message series. She hopes it will inspire you to pray for your future husband—now and forever.

Vee can be contacted at vskripek8@gmail.com.